EXPLAINING CRIMINAL JUSTICE

Steven P. Lab

Marian Williams

Jefferson E. Holcomb

William R. King

Michael E. Buerger

Bowling Green State University

Roxbury Publishing Company
Los Angeles, California

Library of Congress Cataloging-in-Publication Data
Explaining Criminal Justice / Steven P. Lab ... [et al.].
p. cm.
ISBN 1-931719-16-0
1. Criminal justice, Administration of—United States. 2. Criminal
   behavior—United States. 3. Juvenile justice, Administration of—
   United States. 4. Law enforcement—United States. 5. Corrections—
   United States. I. Lab, Steven P.

HV9950.E96 2003
364.973—dc21   2003043220
                                                CIP

EXPLAINING CRIMINAL JUSTICE

Publisher: Claude Teweles
Managing Editor: Dawn VanDercreek
Production Editor: Stephanie Villavicencio Trkay
Copy Editor: Ann West
Proofreader: Scott Oney, Josh Levine
Cover Design: Marnie Kenney
Typography: SDS Design, info@sdsdesign.com

Printed on acid-free paper in the United States of America. This book meets
the standards of recycling of the Environmental Protection Agency.

ISBN 1-931719-16-0

ROXBURY PUBLISHING COMPANY
P.O. Box 491044
Los Angeles, California 90049-9044
Voice: (310) 473-3312 • Fax: (310) 473-4490
Email: roxbury@roxbury.net
Website: www.roxbury.net

Contents

Chapter 4

Courts and Legal Issues 81

Chapter 6
The Juvenile Justice System 137

About the Authors

Steven P. Lab (Ph.D., Florida State University) is a Professor of Criminal Justice and Chair of the Department of Human Services at Bowling Green State University. He is currently the President of the Academy of Criminal Justice Sciences (2003–2004). He teaches courses in the areas of crime prevention and juvenile justice. His current research interests focus mainly on the state of the evidence on what works in crime prevention.

Marian Williams (Ph.D., Florida State University) is an Assistant Professor of Criminal Justice at Bowling Green State University. She teaches courses in criminal courts; criminal procedure; and race, class, and gender. Her research interests include criminal law and procedure, the death penalty, and social justice.

Jefferson E. Holcomb (Ph.D., Florida State University) is an Assistant Professor of Criminal Justice at Bowling Green State University. He has taught undergraduate courses on probation and parole, intermediate sanctions, crime prevention, and research methods. In addition, he teaches graduate courses on corrections, research methods, and criminal justice ethics.

William R. King (Ph.D., University of Cincinnati) is an Assistant Professor of Criminal Justice at Bowling Green State University in Ohio. He teaches courses in policing, criminal justice organizations and management, and criminal justice systems. His research interests include the comparative study of police organizations, applying life-course theory to police agencies, and discretionary decision-making by police officers.

Michael E. Buerger (Ph.D., Rutgers University) is an Associate Professor of Criminal Justice at Bowling Green State University, where he teaches courses in policing, crime prevention, and the nature of crime. He has alternated between the practice and the study of policing throughout his career, with special interest in the dynamic tension between organizational reform and cultural resistance within the ranks. ✦

Chapter One

Crime and the Criminal Justice System

Key Concepts and Terms

- Anonymity
- Confidentiality
- Crime Control
- Dark Figure of Crime
- Deterrence
- Deviance
- Discretion
- Due Process
- Due Process Revolution
- Rehabilitation
- Retribution

Introduction: What Is Crime?

Measuring Crime

To understand crime, it is probably best to start with the notion of social *deviance*, which refers to behavior or actions generally considered inappropriate by others. Deviant acts can be illegal or they might be perfectly legal even though some people consider such acts "wrong" or "bad." For example, wearing a swimsuit to a college lecture would be viewed as inappropriate by most people, although there might not be a law prohibiting this. Some behaviors are considered deviant no matter where or when they are committed (such as killing another person for no good reason), and other behaviors are deviant only during certain situations (e.g., it is usually appropriate to shout during a sporting event, but not during a religious service). Societies usually keep their members from committing less serious deviance by informal social control, such as frowning or other familiar signs and acts of disapproval.

Serious forms of deviance are usually prohibited by societies through written laws. These laws state the prohibited, deviant behavior, the circumstances that make such behavior illegal, and the possible punishment for violating a law. Criminal offenses can be classified as either felonies or misdemeanors. *Felonies,* such as homicide and robbery, are serious breaches of law that can result in a punishment of more than one year in prison. *Misdemeanors* are less serious crimes, such as simple assault and theft, that usually carry a maximum punishment of less than one year in jail. Within the categories of felony and misdemeanor, crimes may be further classified. For example, in Ohio, serious felonies are labeled from felony ones (very serious) to felony fives (less serious). Likewise, misdemeanors are labeled from misdemeanor ones to misdemeanor fours. Other states' exact ranking of their felonies and misdemeanors differ. Regardless of the exact classification scheme, however, when someone engages in such an illegal act, he has broken the law and has thus committed a crime. Therefore, crime occurs when someone commits an act prohibited by a law.

Crime is obviously central to the existence of any criminal justice system, and measuring crime accurately is important. For most places, such as cities and states, crime is expressed as a *crime rate* per 1,000 or 100,000 people per year. For example, a city with a population of 250,000 people in which 3 people were murdered last year would report a homicide rate of 1.2 homicides per 100,000 population. Unfortunately, the true crime rate, sometimes called the *dark figure of crime,* is difficult to measure accurately, so crime rates are often an estimation of the actual number of crimes. Estimating the crime rate can be accomplished by using three methods: official (reported) statistics, self-report statistics, and victimization statistics. All three methods have benefits and disadvantages.

Official Statistics. Official crime statistics are gathered from police agencies, and these statistics represent the total number of crimes (or certain crime types, such as homicide) reported to the police or the number of arrests made by a certain agency. The largest and best known sources of official statistics in the United States are the Federal Bureau of Investigation's (FBI's) Uniform Crime Reports (UCR) and National Incident-Based Reporting System (NIBRS). For further information about these sources, see Maltz (1999) for a discussion of the UCR and Rantala (2000) for discussion of NIBRS. The FBI also compiles data on U.S. homicides into a source known as the Supplemental Homicide Reports (SHR).

If these data are gathered from a police agency, a reasonable estimate of the number of crimes reported to the police can be achieved. In some instances, the total number of arrests or citations made by the police are reported. It is important to remember, however, that official statistics are imperfect measures of crime (especially less serious crime). First, a police agency can increase or decrease the number of arrests, regardless of the true crime rate. For example, a police agency may deploy many officers in a red-light district in order to crack down on prostitution. This crackdown may yield a considerable increase in arrests for prostitution, though the true incidence of prostitution has not changed. Similarly, crimes reported to the police represent just that-crimes in which someone notified his or her victimization and the police chose to record it as a victimization. Research indicates that about one-third of crime victims never report their victimization to the police (Maguire & Pastore, 1997, Table 3.32). Likewise, in some instances people may report a victimization to the police, but that agency may not record the incident as a crime. Overall, the way agencies arrive at official statistics allows a peek at the dark figure of crime. If the crime is not reported, the police do not make an arrest, or the police choose to not record an incident as a crime, then official statistics will not provide an accurate estimate of the true crime rate.

Self-Report Statistics. Self-report statistics overcome some of the limitations of official statistics. These are gathered by asking individuals to report the number of times they have committed a crime during a set period in the past. For example, since 1977, the National Youth Survey (NYS) has surveyed youths and their parents about a range of attitudes and activities, including illegal activities such as alcohol and drug use. The NYS represents one form of self-report statistic about crime. The respondents are usually promised *confidentiality* (i.e., their responses will not be reported to the police) or *anonymity* (the reports cannot be linked to any individual). For example, one could ask high school seniors how many times they have smoked marijuana during the past year. In this way, self-reports avoid some problems associated with official statistics, because it is highly unlikely that most people would be arrested while smoking marijuana or that someone would report marijuana smoking to the police. Self-report statistics are good at tapping less serious offenses.

Unfortunately, there are problems associated with self-report statistics. First, respondents may exaggerate or underreport their criminal behavior. Respondents may exaggerate their criminal activity in order to reinforce their self-concept of being a tough character. Conversely, respondents may underreport because they forgot their criminal activities, because they did not know that what they had done was illegal, or because they are afraid to reveal their past criminal behavior. Finally, *who* are surveyed about their criminal activity is important. For example, giving a self-report survey to high school seniors at their high school is likely to lead one to underestimate the true incidence of crime committed by 17- and 18-year-olds. The serious criminals in this age range are more likely to have been suspended from school, might be skipping school on that day, or might be locked up in a secure juvenile facility. Thus, self-reports also have limitations and do not yield a completely accurate estimate of the true crime rate.

Victimization Studies. The third type of crime statistic comes from victimization studies, which ask people if they have been a victim of a crime during a time period in the past. The National Crime Victimization Survey (NCVS) is a nationally representative survey of U.S. households that is designed to measure criminal victimization. The survey is conducted annually by the Bureau of the Census for the Department of Justice's Bureau of Justice Statistics. As with self-report studies, victimization studies sometimes encounter problems when respondents forget about their victimizations, lie, or fail to tell the interviewer about their victimization. Sometimes, victims will "telescope" a victimization from outside the survey time span. For example, a victimization survey may be concerned only with crimes committed during 2002, but a respondent may report that an assault that he or she actually experienced during 2001 occurred during 2002.

The Philosophies of the Criminal Justice System

The criminal justice system represents society's response to the problem of crime and disorder. At first blush, this seems a clear undertaking; the criminal justice system should fight crime. Yet, *how* society should address its crime problem is not quite as simple. On closer examination, however, one quickly realizes that the system's response to crime is indeed guided by a philosophy about what the system *should* do. There are three such guiding philosophies in criminal justice.

Retribution

Simply, *retribution* is a philosophy based on the belief that criminals should be punished because they have violated the law. Thus, the criminal justice system exists to punish wrongdoers. Punishment should be commensurate with the harm committed by the criminal (an "eye for an eye"). Retribution does not punish to prevent (via deterrence) other potential criminals from committing crime. Regardless of its effectiveness in preventing crime (called *just deserts*), retribution argues that punishment is the proper and just thing for a society to do.

Deterrence

The philosophy of deterrence is related to that of retribution because both advocate punishing criminals. Unlike retribution, however, *deterrence* contends that the proper application of punishment should prevent criminals from future crime by frightening them or making the costs of crime too great. Deterrence argues that the costs of crime (in the form of punishment) must be designed to outweigh the benefits of crime. When potential offenders realize that committing crime is too costly, they will abstain from crime. Deterrence comes in two forms: specific and general. *Specific deterrence* refers to the deterrent effect of punishing a particular offender. For example, a juvenile punished for skipping school will not skip again, for he will remember the punishment he received the first time. *General deterrence* intends to keep people from committing crime by showing them through the experiences of other punished criminals that crime does not pay. Thus, the friends of the juvenile who skipped school will be less likely to skip school in the future, because they learned of the punishment received by their friend for skipping. In this perspective, one does not need to be punished firsthand in order for general deterrence to prevent crime.

Effective deterrence requires three things: *certainty, severity,* and *celerity.* To deter, offenders must be punished every time they commit a crime (certainty). Furthermore, the punishment must be aversive enough to make the punishment outweigh the benefits or fruits of the crime (severity). Finally, the punishment must be inflicted soon after the crime is committed (celerity).

Rehabilitation

Rehabilitation does not advocate punishing criminals, but rather seeks to prevent crime by rectifying problems that are thought to be responsible for the criminal behavior. Examples of rehabilitation include drug treatment, mental health counseling, and job training. Rehabilitation assumes that criminals can be reformed and that, once reformed, they will no longer engage in crime. Thus, according to this perspective, the best way for society to combat crime is through treatment and reformation. For more information about rehabilitation, see Cullen and Gilbert (1989).

A System of Checks and Balances

To fully appreciate the nature of criminal justice in the United States, take a moment to compare the current system to other systems of criminal justice. Perhaps some persons have wished that a criminal justice system should not be necessary. Indeed, some utopian societies have tried this, although they have still exercised informal social control to keep their members in line. By contrast, some societies have created extremely oppressive criminal justice systems, in which citizens have no rights and the power of the state to arrest, charge, and imprison is almost absolute (e.g., Nazi Germany and its secret police, the Gestapo). These two extreme examples of how societies might fashion their criminal justice systems help one appreciate the uniqueness of criminal justice in the United States.

The first important characteristic of criminal justice in the United States is that our system represents a balance among several opposing forces. First, the system tries to balance the right of people to do what they want (*individual liberty*) with the requirement that society remain civil, calm, and relatively crime free (*societal civility*). Thus, the state imposes restrictions on individual behavior through laws and the agencies designed to enforce them in an attempt to keep society orderly. This desire for order must be balanced, however, with the people's desire for freedom to do what they want. If there is too much governmental restriction, people are oppressed by their government and its agents (police, courts, corrections). On the other hand, if there are too few restrictions, society can veer toward disorder and chaos. But liberty and civility are not the only forces to be balanced in criminal justice.

Writing in 1968, Herbert Packer noted that the criminal justice system also balances the competing philosophies of crime control and due process in its operations. *Crime control* advocates the aggressive and quick apprehension, trial, and processing of criminals. It cares less about ensuring that suspects are given specific legal rights than that the system will efficiently process suspects to suppress crime. In contrast, *due process* contends that suspects should be given copious rights and that the system should carefully ensure that these rights are not violated by the system. In other words, a due process perspective is concerned less with suppressing crime than with ensuring that individuals are not unfairly harmed by their government. Although the criminal justice system tries to balance these competing philosophies, in reality it constantly swings between the two extremes.

Balancing competing ideologies also applies to the philosophies of criminal justice (retribution, deterrence, rehabilitation). The system constantly oscillates among such philosophies and, in many cases, decisions made to satisfy more than one ideology. Yet, this constant mixture of philosophies means that advocates of one philosophy (e.g., retribution) are never completely happy, for the system never fully implements their version of justice. Instead, the system is operating under all three philosophies in most situations. A mix of philosophies is sometimes evident when individual criminal justice employees make decisions. For example, judges might decide upon a defendant's sentence length based upon the amount of time required for rehabilitation, but they may also decide to simultaneously punish the offender and to send a deterrent message to the community. Probation can be viewed as a way for the state to keep offenders under surveillance in their community (thus achieving a degree of deterrence) while also requiring treatment or counseling for them (thus providing rehabilitation). In action, then, the criminal justice system cannot be viewed as being committed to any one philosophy. Rather, the operation of the system is a simultaneous combination of these different ideologies.

Unlike in many nations where there is one national criminal justice system, criminal justice in the United States is composed of many loosely coupled, semiautonomous organizations. For example, instead of one national police force, over 20,000 police agencies act as separate, independent agencies. Likewise, instead of one court system, there are both state and federal courts. Cities and towns also have municipal courts that operate under local rules of procedure.

This loosely coupled system reflects Americans' distrust of large government and their preference for local control, and it also facilitates a system of checks and balances. In some states, certain criminal justice positions are elected (e.g., sheriffs, judges, chief prosecutors), but other positions are appointed by elected officials (e.g., assistant prosecutors, parole board). In this way, citizens exercise local control over their criminal justice system. This system also facilitates a system of checks and balances, in which the decisions of one criminal justice agency are reviewed (and corrected if necessary) by subsequent criminal justice agencies. For example, prosecutors usually conduct a pretrial screening with arrestees to decide if charges will be pressed or the case dropped. In effect, prosecutors review the work of police officers responsible for an arrest and decide if the suspect should be charged. The separation of components of the criminal justice process facilitates the review of decisions. Likewise, the decision to charge is not the final decision. Judges will have the opportunity to review this decision and, if the case goes to trial, either a judge or jury will further evaluate the defendant's guilt. In this way, then, loosely coupled agencies check the decisions made by other agencies. Although it may appear cumbersome and inefficient at times to have so many different agencies dispensing justice, this system does protect citizens from a single, all-powerful state.

The Four C's of the Criminal Justice System (Citizens, Cops, Courts, and Corrections)

The American criminal justice system can be viewed as a conglomeration of loosely coupled organizations, each processing the outputs of the previous agency. The system can also be viewed as a process model, whereby decisions made by one system component influence the following components. The process model is detailed below to further an understanding of how the system works in reality. This system model can be called "the Four C's of the Criminal Justice System." The process model also highlights the importance of decision making (which encompasses *discretion*) by individuals in the system. Figure 1.1 portrays this process model of criminal justice (Bureau of Justice Statistics, 1997).

The first component of the system's C's refers to people not employed by the system: citizens. Although they are not part of the system, citizens, as victims and offenders, make decisions that are crucial for understanding how the system works. That is, citizens provide the vast majority of inputs for the rest of the system. Research indicates that most people are arrested because another citizen has complained to the police about that person (in effect, reporting a crime or disturbance). Research indicates that, even when victimized, people do not always call the police to report a crime. In fact, only one-third to one-half of crime victims report their victimization to the police. This rate of reporting varies depending on the crime type. For example, roughly 76 percent of vehicle theft victims report their loss to the police, whereas only about 28 percent of theft victims report their victimization. Thus, it is important to remember that the police are often reliant on citizen reports of crime, and citizens do not always tell the police about their victimizations.

The second decision-making node of the system consists of the police. Police officers do not patrol the streets arresting everyone suspected of committing a crime; rather, officers selectively enforce the law. In many instances, an officer chooses *not* to arrest, even when there is probable cause to make an arrest. Not fully enforcing all the laws all the time is a good thing; society would probably not tolerate full enforcement of every law. Again, the police exercise considerable discretion about the situations in which to get involved and the ways to resolve these situations. The police decision to arrest is thus influenced by the seriousness of the suspected offense, the wishes of the victim (i.e., does the victim want the suspect arrested or does he or she request leniency), and the expressed attitude of the suspect (called *demeanor*). In the majority of cases, however, the police do not make an arrest.

The third decision node is composed of court workers (pretrial intake workers, prosecutors, defense attorneys, and judges) and is

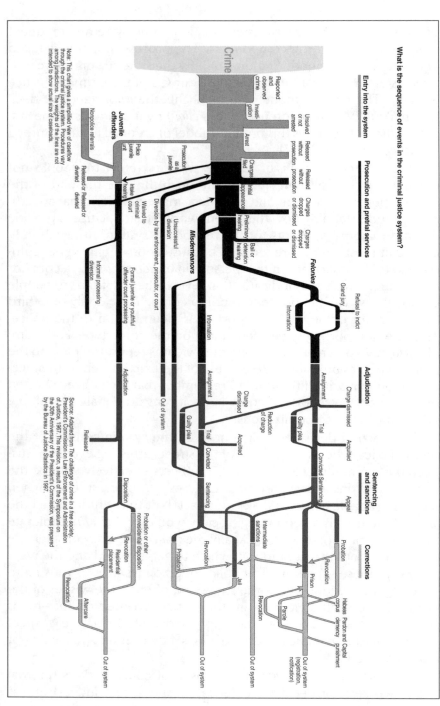

Figure 1.1

often referred to as the *courtroom workgroup*. Not all persons in the courtroom workgroup are employed by a particular court, nor are they necessarily employed by the criminal justice system (e.g., defendants may employ their own defense attorney who is not employed by the government, but is a member of the workgroup). Thus, courtroom decisions are not made by members of the same organization, but rather by a range of actors who meet in a court "arena" and work with suspects brought to them by the police. These workgroup members exercise considerable discretion about a range of decisions. Prosecutors can decide to dismiss a case outright, reduce the charges, accept a guilty plea, or proceed to trial. Likewise, defendants and defense attorneys can decide to accept a plea agreement or hold out for a trial. Finally, judges make important decisions concerning the admissibility of evidence, the verdict, and sentencing.

The final decision node is composed of criminal justice system employees who work in corrections. It includes probation and parole officers, correctional and detention officers, and those who provide services to offenders (e.g., social workers providing substance abuse or employment counseling). These professionals make relevant decisions about the exact conditions of probationers' and parolees' supervision, such as how many office or home visits will be required, whether or not probationers or parolees will be drug tested, and how violations of supervision will be handled. Likewise, correctional and detention officers make decisions about whether to write up rule violations. Inmates may be punished for committing crimes while in prison or violating prison rules. Likewise, probationers and parolees can be sentenced to prison or jail if they violate the conditions of their supervision or commit a new crime while under supervision.

Recent Trends in Criminal Justice

Like all social systems, the criminal justice system has undergone changes over its history. The following four significant changes that have occurred since the early 1960s emphasize how the criminal justice system is influenced by trends and changes in our society.

The first recent change in criminal justice began during the early 1960s and has been termed the *due process revolution*. This trend originated when a number of court cases were decided in ways that provided the public and those accused of committing crime with greater protections from the government. In particular, the U.S. Supreme Court ruled during the 1960s that arrestees could have an attorney present during questioning and that the police had to notify arrestees of this fact (*Miranda v. Arizona,* 1966). Later court rulings provided additional protections to prisoners and probationers. For example, prisoners were granted wider freedoms concerning freedom of speech and religion while incarcerated. Likewise, adults under community supervision were given due process protections during probation and parole revocation hearings. Taken together, the due process revolution limited the power of the state over its citizens and, hence, afforded greater protections to citizens, suspects, and prisoners.

The second recent trend in criminal justice has been the civil rights movement and, most important, the increased representation of people of color and women as criminal justice employees. Historically, even until the late 1960s, criminal justice employees had almost always been white males. As the civil rights movement gained momentum in the United States, the system began to open employment opportunities to minorities. For example, many city police agencies began actively recruiting African Americans as police officers during the mid- to late 1960s. Likewise, prisons and probation and parole departments also recruited and hired minorities in attempts to make the system's employees more representative of the country's population. This recent development is due in large part to the broader civil rights movement.

The third recent trend in criminal justice has been the inclusion of *community* in many facets of the system. Since the mid-1980s, for example, various aspects of the system have sought to include the views, opinions, input, and even assistance of local community members. Such was not always the case. Outcomes of this criminal justice trend are community policing, changes in community corrections (i.e., probation and parole), and the creation of special drug courts. Alternatives to traditional courts, such as *alternative dispute resolution,* are also represented here, for they change the role that community members and victims play in criminal justice processes. Overall, community-oriented changes have involved victims and community residents as a way to tailor local criminal justice responses to each locale.

A fourth trend that influenced the criminal justice system during the past thirty years is the increasingly punitive response to crime and drug use. The "tough on crime" approach that began in the early 1970s was a response to the perceived leniency of so-called liberal policies toward problems of social order during the 1960s. This "law and order" response resulted in dramatic increases in the number of persons arrested and imprisoned for drug use and increased the severity of punishment for a number of offenses. Many restrictions on police practices that had been established in the 1960s were relaxed in favor of giving more power to the police. Sentencing guidelines enacted by many legislatures restricted the discretion of judges to impose sentences. In particular, the use of mandatory and presumptive prison sentences for certain offenses increased the number and length of prison sentences. Furthermore, some states abolished parole in order to keep offenders incarcerated for longer periods of time.

As a result, these and other policies have dramatically increased the number of offenders handled by the criminal justice system. This is especially true for correctional facilities, which have seen a fourfold increase in the incarceration rate since 1973 (Blumstein & Beck, 1999). Hence, many agencies have noted dramatic increases in their budgets and have been pressured to change their organizational behavior to be consistent with political mandates for more punitive responses to crime and offenders.

References

Blumstein, A., & Beck, A. (1999). Population growth in U.S. prisons, 1980–1996. In M. Tonry and J. Petersilia (Eds.), *Prisons* (pp. 17–61). Chicago: University of Chicago Press.

Cullen, F. T., & Gilbert, K. (1989). *Reaffirming rehabilitation.* Cincinnati, OH: Anderson Publishing.

Maguire, K., & Pastore, A. L. (1997). *Sourcebook of criminal justice statistics 1996.* Washington, DC: U.S. Department of Justice.

Maltz, M. D. (1999). *Bridging gaps in police crime data: A discussion paper from the BJS Fellows Program.* Washington, DC: U.S. Department of Justice.

Miranda v. Arizona, 384 U.S. 436 (1966).

Packer, H. (1968). *The limits of the criminal sanction.* Stanford, CA: Stanford University Press.

Rantala, R. (2000). *Effects of NIBRS on crime statistics.* Washington, DC: Bureau of Justice Statistics Special Report.

U.S. Department of Justice, Bureau of Justice Statistics. (1997). What is the sequence of events in the criminal justice system? Retrieved September 3, 2002, from *www.ojp.usdoj.gov/bjs/largechart.htm.*

Suggested Readings

History of the Criminal Justice System

Johnson, H. A., & Wolfe, N. T. (1996). *History of criminal justice* (2nd Ed.). Cincinnati, OH: Anderson Publishing.

History of American Criminal Justice

Walker, S. (1998). *Popular justice: A history of American criminal justice* (2nd Ed.). New York: Oxford University Press.

Discretionary Decision Making in the Criminal Justice System

Gottfredson, M., & Gottfredson, D. (1988). *Decision making in criminal justice: Toward the rational exercise of discretion.* New York: Plenum.

Discussion Questions

1. Which philosophy of the criminal justice system do you feel is most appropriate and why? Does it matter what the specific offense is that an offender is charged with (e.g., drug offense, property offense, etc.) or who the offender is (e.g., drug addict, juvenile offender, repeat offender, etc.)? Why?

2. What do you think are the difficulties in balancing the due process and crime control models in criminal justice in the United States? ✦

Chapter Two

Theories and Explanations of Crime

Key Concepts and Terms

- Anomie
- Ecological Fallacy
- Biosocial Theories
- Chicago School
- Classicism
- Conflict Theories
- Developmental Theories
- Differential Association
- Ecological Perspective
- Genetic Theories
- Labeling Perspective
- Learning Theories
- MMPI
- Modeling
- Modes of Adaptation
- Neoclassicism
- Operant Conditioning

- Operationalization
- Personality Theories
- Physical Appearance Theories
- Positivism
- Psychoanalytic Theories
- Rational Choice Theory
- Routine Activities
- Self-Control Theory
- Social Control Theory
- Social Disorganization
- Social Learning Theories
- Strain Theories
- Subcultural Theories
- Techniques of Neutralization
- Theory
- Theory Integration

Introduction

Any discussion of criminal justice or crime invariably rests on assumptions about the causes of criminal activity. This is true in even the most basic arguments that people have about what society should do about crime. Should society get tough on criminals and increase the level of punishment or should it take a more rehabilitative approach and work with offenders to overcome their problems? The answers inevitably hinge on what the parties to the argument think causes crime. Most often, however, people do not consciously realize they are making assumptions about causes of behavior. What they are doing, without knowing it, is relying on theories to drive their discussions.

Many people shrink from discussions of theory, however, because they believe this is an esoteric exercise that has no use in the real world. They may assume that this is something only philosophers or specially trained individuals can undertake. The reality is that everyone theorizes every day. A *theory* is nothing more than an attempt to answer the question Why? Why did someone act the way he did? Why did the accident occur? Why is the economy in trouble? Many such questions arise throughout the day for every individual, and any attempt to give an explanation is a theory.

Both criminal justice and criminology seek to test theories explaining the causes of crime and the effectiveness of various crime interventions. Ideally, any interventions are based on theories that have been previously supported by research. Theories of criminality attempt to establish that certain factors (i.e., the independent variables) exert a causal influence on criminal behavior (i.e., the dependent variable). To demonstrate that a causal relationship exists between two factors or variables, three criteria must be met. The first is known as *correlation,* which can be characterized as follows: when one variable changes, there is a corresponding change in the other variable. For example, if the unemployment rate increases and there is a corresponding increase in the crime rate, a correlation exists between the unemployment rate (the independent variable) and the crime rate (the dependent variable).

The second criterion needed to establish a causal relationship is *time order.* This means that the independent variable (which influences change) must temporally precede the dependent variable (which is changed by the effect of the independent variable). For example, if a researcher is examining the effect of the unemployment rate on the crime rate, then the unemployment rate must change before the crime rate changes. Part of a good theory is an explicit assumption about the time order between the two variables.

The final requirement, and often the most difficult to demonstrate, is a *lack of spuriousness.* A spurious variable is one that affects the independent and dependent variables and is the variable or factor actually responsible for the originally observed relationship. For example, funding for social services may influence both the unemployment rate and the crime rate, and it may explain the original relationship between the unemployment rate and the crime rate. Well-designed tests of theories and interventions attempt to consider all possible spurious variables and control their influence when looking at the relationship between the independent and dependent variables. Most theories attempt to identify and discount these alternative causes in the initial explanation. It is up to research, however, to demonstrate that all three factors (correlation, time order, and lack of spuriousness) are present when attempting to validate a theory.

An additional difficulty in conducting social research is the operationalization of the key variables of each theory or intervention. *Operationalization* is the process of taking an abstract concept (such as "crime" or "unemployment") and turning it into a measurable variable for analysis. Unlike the physical sciences, the social sciences have few, if any, universally agreed upon measures for important theoretical concepts. For example, the "crime rate" could be measured as the number of arrests (per 100,000 population) reported by police in the Uniform Crime Reports *or* the number of victimizations (per 100,000 population) reported by citizens in the National Crime Victimization Survey (which, in many cases, are not reported to the police). Chapter 1 identified many of the problems associated with measuring crime, and problems exist for the measurement of a variety of other social phenomena, such as "friendships" and "social supports." Differing measurements of a single variable make it difficult to provide conclusive evidence of a proposed theory. The result is that any test of a theory or social intervention is limited by the *validity* (accuracy) and *reliability* (consistency) of the measurements of the variables of interest. Thus, no single test is thought to be conclusive. Instead, social research proceeds on the basis of building upon previous studies and of refining various measures of crime and criminal justice.

In criminal justice and criminology, there are many theories. These theories range from explanations of why individuals commit crimes to why a society outlaws certain behaviors and why the criminal justice system responds the way it does to crime. Most discussions in criminal justice theory revolve around the question of why people act the way they do. These are the theories of criminal behavior. This chapter provides a brief introduction to the development of criminological theories and an overview of the major theories of criminal behavior. Included in the chapter are discussions of biological, psychological, and sociological theories, with the greatest emphasis placed on the latter group, because of their prominence in most criminological discussions.

Theoretical Schools of Thought

Every theory of behavior involves implicit assumptions about individuals and the society in which they operate. In addition, every scientific area has schools of thought within which certain theories are developed. In criminology, the two major schools of thought are classicism and positivism.

The Classical School

Classicism views human beings as free-willed and *hedonistic* (i.e., maximizing pleasure and minimizing pain). Individuals make free choices about what to do based on what they perceive as bringing about the greatest amount of pleasure with the least amount of pain. Crime, therefore, results from a person choosing to violate the law because he believes that there is a level of benefit to be derived from the action. The individual is not forced by circumstances or situations to break the law. Instead, the person freely chooses a course of action.

Based on the assumption of free-willed behavior, the classical school believes that the key to solving crime is to alter the hedonistic calculation that people make when opting for one mode of behavior over another. The solution to crime, therefore, is to decrease the amount of pleasure or increase the level of pain, or both, that a person receives from acting a certain way. The result would be that individuals would refrain from those behaviors that fail to bring about more pleasure than pain. On the basis of these assumptions, Cesare Beccaria, an early proponent of classicism, argued that the solution to crime requires establishing and enforcing laws and penalties for unwanted behaviors. Individuals would then know the consequences for different behaviors and could make informed choices about what to do and what not to do. He argued that individuals would be deterred from committing crime because of the fear of punishment that would follow from such actions.

The Positivist School

Positivism takes a very different approach to understanding behavior and what should be done to alter behavior. Rather than believing in free will, positivism rests on *determinism*, or the belief that a person's actions are dictated by forces beyond his control. Everything a person does, both deviant and conventional, is determined for the individual. The challenge is to identify what the causes are and to intervene in them. Unfortunately, there is no single cause for crime or for even a specific type of crime. Positivism argues that there are multiple causes for behavior that vary from person to person and from crime to crime. In order to identify the specific cause(s) at work at any given time, positivists approach criminal behavior in a fashion similar to that of a doctor who is working with a sick patient. This *medical model* looks at crime as a symptom of underlying causes that must be identified before a proper response is formulated. Once the underlying causes for the crime are identified, the appropriate treatment can be implemented. *Treatment* and *rehabilitation* are the cornerstones of positivism. Punishment will not work because the individual does not choose to commit crime. Rather, some form of intervention must be applied to ameliorate the causes of the crime and keep the individual from further criminal activity.

Neoclassicism

Today, neither classicism nor positivism dominates thinking about criminal behavior. Instead, a hybrid version of the two has emerged. *Neoclassicism* takes the approach that most individuals exercise some degree of free will. At the same time, the choices that an individual has are limited by various factors, such as the economic conditions of the community, family background, and the innate abilities of the individual. Thus, individuals can make decisions only on the basis of what is available to them. This is referred to as *soft-determinism*. The causes of crime, therefore, can include a mix of both free-willed choice and factors beyond the control of the individual. Consequently, the response to criminal behavior must be multifaceted. Although a belief in free will dominates in today's deterrence explanations, most theoretical explanations fall more into the realm of positivism or neoclassicism. Therefore, the balance of this chapter addresses theories that reflect primarily one of these perspectives.

Biological Explanations

The earliest theories of behavior focused almost exclusively on biological factors. Even though discussions of biological factors have persisted throughout the years, they were largely discounted in the late nineteenth century and took a backseat to psychological and sociological theories throughout the twentieth century. In recent years, however, biological explanations have begun to reappear as our ability to examine and understand the biological functioning of the human body has improved.

Physical Appearance Theories

Early biological theories attempted to identify criminals by the way they looked. *Physiognomy* proposed that facial features were related to behavior, and *phrenology* argued that the shape of the skull (including the facial features) could explain how a person acted. Although these approaches appear simplistic, they came from an underlying assumption (particularly in phrenology) that the brain was responsible for behavior and the shape of one's head dictated cranial capacity. Thus, the real interest was not in how a person looked, but in what those looks meant for the ability of the brain to dictate activity.

The basic ideas of physical appearance received their greatest support from the work of Cesare Lombroso. Lombroso, often considered the father of modern criminology, based his ideas on Charles Darwin's survival of the species. According to Lombroso, individuals who committed crimes were acting more in concert with animal instincts of self-preservation and individual need than were individuals who avoided deviant behavior. Deviant individuals were less evolved physically and mentally than nondeviants and could be identified by the *atavistic* (in this case ape-like) qualities they displayed (1876). Lombroso's work was heavily attacked, challenged especially by his attempts to compare criminals with noncriminals in terms of their atavistic traits. In most of those comparisons, however, more similarities than dissimilarities were found between the criminals and noncriminals. Today, Lombroso's work is noted more for his attempt to develop a scientific explanation for behavior than for the explanation he offered.

Despite the criticisms of physical appearance theories, they continued to appear throughout the twentieth century. Perhaps the most cited efforts have been those of Sheldon and the Gluecks. Sheldon (1949) identified three basic *somatotypes* or body types and attempted to show that individuals of one type were more criminal than those of another. What distinguished his work was the fact that he coupled each body type with a corresponding temperament, which helped explain behavior. The most criminal type of individual had a *mesomorphic* build (muscular, barrel-chested) with a *somotonic* temperament (dynamic, aggressive, active). The least criminal individual had an *ectomorphic* physique (thin, bony, delicate) and a *cerebrotonic* temperament (nervous, introvert). Between these two extremes was the *endomorph,* who was short, fat, and soft, with a *viscerotonic* temperament (easygoing, extrovert). Sheldon (1949), as well as Glueck and Glueck (1956), found a predominance of mesomorphs and few ectomorphs among incarcerated male juveniles. Unfortunately, the analyses failed to take into account the fact that a person's build and temperament may change over time and due to circumstances, such as being incarcerated. Although physical appearance theories still pop up from time to time, they have given way to other biological theories for behavior.

Genetics and Inheritance Explanations

The idea that criminal tendencies are inherited appears in many of the early physical appearance studies of crime. This was a logical extension of the recognition that many physical features are passed on from generation to generation. The primary debate in genetic explanations is over the relative influence of genetics and the environment. This is referred to as the *nature versus nurture controversy.* The problem has always been to divide the influence of nature from that of nurture in order to see what is most important. Two primary approaches have been used to address this issue: studies of twins and studies of adoption. Twin studies look at the differences between *monozygotic* (identical) twins and *dizygotic* (fraternal) twins. If behavior is genetically determined, monozygotic twins should display high levels of similar behavior when compared with dizygotic twins. Research on twins shows more similarity in behavior among identical twins, but the similarity is not perfect. The concern with this research is that there is no control over the environment in which the twins are raised. Adoption studies seek to address the problem of separating the genetic components from the environmental influences by examining offspring who have been adopted compared with their biological parents and families. The assumption is that the adoption places the infant in a different environment from that of the parent. Any similarity in parent-child behavior, therefore, should be attributable to genetics. Again, research shows support for the genetic argument, with greater similarity between the adoptees and their biological families.

The relationship in both twin and adoption studies, however, is not absolute, and there are probably more environmental factors at work than there are genetic components. What cannot be discounted is the fact that some genetic influence is at work. Despite these findings, genetic explanations have had little direct impact on the operations of the criminal justice system. Exceptions to this include the use of findings that show genetic propensities for alcoholism, schizophrenia, and other problems. This information can be used to screen individuals for risk and possibly offer early interventions. As genetic science continues to progress, it is probable that the criminal justice system will have to adjust its policies accordingly.

Biosocial Approaches

Some of the most recent theories advanced for deviant behavior involve biological factors. A big difference between these new theories and those discussed above is the recognition that the biological factors do not occur in a vacuum. Rather, it is the intersection of biological factors with the larger environment that may lead to criminal and deviant behavior. The idea that the biological makeup of the individual interacts with the surrounding environment to influence behavior is known as *biosociology*. Various biosocial arguments have been advanced to explain behavior, including hormonal imbalances, chemical influences, and others.

Hormonal factors refer to the effect on behavior of naturally produced chemicals in the body. Most research in this area focuses on testosterone levels in males and hormonal changes as a result of menstruation in females (see Booth & Osgood, 1993; Dalton, 1964; Reiss & Roth, 1993). Both the testosterone and premenstrual syndrome explanations suffer from a variety of shortcomings, especially the lack of good empirical analyses. In both cases, however, there is evidence that these hormonal factors play some role in behavior.

Not only do naturally produced chemicals possibly influence behavior; so does the introduction of chemicals in the body. Two common groups of substances receive attention in relation to criminal behavior: alcohol and drugs. The existence of a link between these substances and crime is indisputable. What is not known is exactly *how* they influence behavior. Interestingly, sugar is another substance that has received a great deal of study in relation to crime. The basic argument has been that excessively high sugar levels make a person irritable and may lead to aggressive activity. This view is also used by many parents to explain the hyperactivity of their children. Although a great deal of research has examined the influence of sugar on behavior, most of the research has been poorly done and has failed to find any clear link between sugar and deviant behavior (Gray & Gray, 1983).

Numerous additional biosocial factors are emerging as potential explanations for behavior. One area of study involves the influence of *neurotransmitters* (chemicals that assist in the transmission of electrical impulses in the central nervous system). Early research on this topic found a definite relationship between some neurotransmitters and deviance (Reiss & Roth, 1993). While still in its infancy, such research reveals that frontal and temporal lobe problems are related to deviant activity (Raine, 1993).

The emergence of biosocial research has reinvigorated interest in biological factors as a cause of criminal and deviant behavior. Arguments from this perspective, however, remain on the edges of most theoretical discussions. This is largely due to the fact that most of the individuals interested in criminal behavior and criminal justice have been trained in either the psychological or the sociological tradition. Thus, biology is usually a foreign topic to those who study criminal behavior. Because of this, biosocial explanations are very slow to be accepted in the field.

Nevertheless, biosocial explanations have influenced the operations of the criminal justice field. In 1979, Dan White argued in court that he was suffering from *diminished mental capacity* when he killed the mayor of San Francisco and another man as a result of eating too much sugar. As a consequence, he was convicted of voluntary manslaughter instead of first-degree murder. In another example, some judges have proscribed drug therapy to reduce the testosterone levels of sexual predators. While these types of actions are not common, they indicate the emerging influence of biosocial arguments in the criminal justice system.

Psychological Explanations

Psychological theories make up a second general approach to explaining criminal and deviant behavior. Early psychological theories had close ties to biological and physical explanations, largely due to the emergence of psychiatry, which seeks physiological explanations for behavior. Most current psychological theories, however, do not look for a physical explanation. Instead, they generally exhibit several other distinctive features. First, they typically look for problems arising out of early life experiences. Second, the explanations are highly individualistic. While similar factors may be at work across numerous individuals, each case must be considered on its own terms. Finally, psychological explanations tend to be more applicable in treatment settings. This is due both to the individualistic nature of most approaches and the fact that these explanations are applied only after an individual has committed a violation.

Psychoanalytic Approaches

Psychoanalysis rests on the premise that unconscious and instinctual factors account for a great deal of an individual's behavior, particularly deviant activity. Sigmund Freud, the most noted name in psychoanalysis, argued that deviance is a direct result of unconscious drives and desires, over which the individual has little direct control. For Freud, the key was to recognize this fact and find ways to exert control over one's behavior.

Freudian psychoanalysis outlines three parts to the personality that are involved in behavior: the id, ego, and superego. The *id* is made up of the unconscious drives and desires of the individual, of which most people are unaware. On the other hand, the *superego* involves the values and moral character of the individual that come from interaction with others and training as the individual grows. The superego may be either conscious or unconscious. The final part of the personality, the *ego*, is the social identity of the individual. It is how a person actually behaves throughout the day. Given these three components, the id and superego are typically at odds over what to do. The id pushes a person to act in a certain way, but the superego says that the desired behavior is socially unacceptable. When this conflict is finally resolved, the resulting behavior reflects the ego.

Deviance is one possible outcome of the conflict between the id and the superego (see Van Voorhis et al., 1997). This may be due to the id winning the conflict and leading a person to deviant activity. Deviance may also result from compromise between the id and superego, in which the original desire is replaced by another one that is also deviant. The goal of psychoanalysis is to make the individual aware of the conflict between the id and superego so that the person can seek out socially acceptable methods for resolving the internal conflict. While numerous attempts to study psychoanalysis have been undertaken, the key concepts of id and superego cannot be measured in any direct way and can be identified only through long and intensive therapy sessions. As a consequence, psychoanalysis is used primarily in treatment settings where the individual is required to participate.

Developmental Explanations

Many psychological explanations portray deviance as a result of interrupted development during childhood. The assumption is that normal development proceeds through a variety of stages, generally beginning with a self-centered view of the world and progressing to a stage in which the individual makes choices in the best interests of both himself and the world. The failure to progress beyond certain stages of development may leave an individual in a situation where decisions are made that result in unacceptable behavior. The key for developmental theories, therefore, is to identify the stage at which an individual is operating and assist him in moving forward to higher developmental levels.

Perhaps the most well known developmental approach for understanding criminal and delinquent behavior uses the *Interpersonal Maturity Levels* (I-levels). The I-levels scale is made up of seven levels that represent progressive development in both social and interpersonal skills. Delinquency and criminality typically appear in individuals who are operating in levels 2 through 4, where the person sees things mainly in relation to what pleasure or good they can bring. Individuals in these levels have not yet developed a sense of how one's actions affect others. Thus, the reference for all behavior tends to be what benefits one's self (Sullivan et al., 1957).

A second well-known developmental approach is Kohlberg's (1981) *moral development theory*. According to Kohlberg's model, six primary stages of development fall into three basic levels: preconventional, conventional, and postconventional. The preconventional level is characterized by concern over one's own comfort, safety, and convenience, but those reaching the conventional level consider both their own and others' concerns and interests, and what is good for society. In the third level, individuals focus mainly on the good of the collective and strive to act according to the highest moral principles. Few individuals reach the final levels of moral development. Deviance and criminality are a consequence of failing to move out of the preconventional level. Once again, the challenge is to get the individuals to move beyond a self-centered view of the world and to operate more in line with socially acceptable behaviors.

Developmental approaches to understanding behavior receive a good deal of acceptance, largely because the ideas are easy to understand and it is easy to see how people change and develop in many different ways throughout their lives. Developmental approaches lend themselves primarily to treatment and rehabilitation and are frequently used as a part of correctional interventions. Clearly, the fact that an individual may not be advancing appropriately through developmental stages is usually recognized only after the person violates the law or otherwise displays deviant tendencies. The response is then to figure out at what stage the individual is and work to move him into more advanced stages of development.

Learning Theories

In one sense, developmental theories are special forms of learning theories. *Learning theories* assume that people learn just about everything from their environment, particularly from the people with whom they have contact. An underlying assumption in many developmental approaches is that people learn what is appropriate behavior and that this knowledge becomes more complex as the individual ages and learns more things.

A wide range of learning theories has been proposed in both the psychological and sociological literature. Perhaps the simplest form of learning is *modeling*. Under this approach, children learn by copying the behavior of others around them, particularly their parents and siblings (Bandura & Walters, 1963). Children can also model the behavior of characters they see on television or in the movies. A more sophisticated psychological learning theory is *operant conditioning*, which focuses on how behavior is reinforced through a system of rewards and punishments. The basic premise is that behavior reinforced with pleasurable feedback is more likely to be repeated, while activities that are punished and bring about painful responses will be avoided in the future (Skinner, 1953). The impact of rewards and punishments has been demonstrated most clearly in studies with animals and more indirectly in research using children and adults. The ability to mold behavior through reward systems has led many institutions to use token economies and similar approaches (discussed in a later chapter) to control the behavior of clients.

Personality Traits

Psychologists have long been interested in identifying whether deviant individuals exhibit different personality traits than other persons. Sheldon and Eleanor Glueck (1950) proposed one of the earlier personality arguments when they claimed to have found differences between delinquents and nondelinquents. According to the Gluecks, personality factors characteristic of delinquents included being more extroverted, impulsive, hostile, assertive, and defiant as well as being less fearful of failure and caring less about authority. These factors could be used to identify potential delinquents for treatment programs. Concerns about their findings, however, revolve primarily around the methods they used in identifying these traits. When choosing delinquents to study, they opted to use 500 male youths incarcerated in a state training school. These youths were compared with 500 youths not in an institution. One major problem with this approach is the fact that the delinquent youths may display these traits as a result of being incarcerated, rather than exhibiting the traits before system contact. A second major concern is the fact that many of the traits are often considered to be desirable in youths, such as being assertive, extroverted, and unafraid to fail. Despite these concerns, the Gluecks' findings have formed the basis of a great deal of subsequent work in the juvenile justice system.

Interest in personality traits has led to the development of standardized instruments for measuring different personality dimensions and traits. A standardized instrument, such as a multiple choice test, has several advantages over the more traditional approach of conducting one-on-one interviews with clients and assessing each person individually. The standardized instrument is more cost-effective and eliminates the bias of individual raters. Perhaps the most recognized approach to uncovering personality traits is the *Minnesota Multiphasic Personality Inventory* (MMPI). The MMPI consists of over 550 true-false questions that measure personality along 10 different dimensions or scales. The inventory was developed using personality dimensions identified and used extensively in clinical settings (Megargee & Bohn, 1979). No single question is used to indicate a personality trait, and no single scale can indicate whether a person is or will be deviant. Instead, the MMPI looks to see patterns of responses that will indicate the likelihood of certain types of behaviors. The MMPI has been applied extensively with offenders, particularly for determining the proper interventions and treatments to use. Less use of the inventory is found outside the institutional settings. In those instances where it has been used with other subjects, there is some evidence of differential results based on the demographic makeup of those taking the test.

There remains a great deal of debate about whether offenders can be identified according to their personality traits. Although individuals displaying extreme behaviors can probably be accurately assessed, the problem is identifying the traits that differentiate the vast majority of people who do not fall into an extreme category. Despite this fact, personality traits are used to identify unknown offenders and to determine profiles of potential offenders. The problem with this is that the identification of personality traits is still in a state of development, and much more research is needed before using these traits to intervene in the lives of people.

Sociological Explanations

Sociological theories examine how the social environment affects a person's behavior. The emphasis is on what is occurring around the individual-with the family, peers, neighborhood, economy, society. Sociological theories have come to dominate most criminological discussions because they are more easily put to empirical testing, are more intuitive and understandable by laypersons, and incorporate more factors into the explanations than psychological theories.

The Ecological Perspective

Ecological explanations shifted attention away from the biological and psychological approaches that dominated at the turn of the twentieth century and ushered in more sociologically oriented explanations. The *ecological perspective,* often referred to as the *Chicago School,* was one of the earliest sociological attempts to explain deviance and borrowed heavily on the ideas of plant ecology. Basically, this approach views crime and deviance as a natural result of the conditions found in certain parts of major cities. The ecological perspective emerged in the early 1900s when U.S. cities in the Northeast and Midwest were experiencing a great deal of population growth as a result of the migration of southern blacks and European immigrants to industrial jobs in these locations. The cities were being inundated with new residents on an almost daily basis, and many recently arrived individuals were poorly educated, did not have the skills to work in the plants, and could not speak English. In order to accommodate this growth, cities were expanding outward, with more wealthy residents moving into better neighborhoods and leaving the older, more run-down areas to the poor immigrants.

Two early researchers, Shaw and McKay (1942), examined where crime and delinquency were taking place in Chicago and found that most deviance occurred in the same areas, year after year. Even when the population of the areas changed, the crime stayed in the same place. In describing those areas, the authors noted that they were poor areas populated by recent immigrants to the city. They also noted a constant turnover in the population, mainly due to the desire of people to relocate in better neighborhoods as soon as they could afford to move. This turnover caused a problem that Shaw and McKay (1942) called *social disorganization*. Basically, this meant that the people in these areas did not, or could not, exert control over what was taking place in the neighborhood. The residents were mainly interested in bettering their own situation so they could move out. This lack of concern for the area allowed crime and delinquency to run unchecked.

The basic ideas of the ecological approach have been found in research conducted in a variety of other cities and are still used today. That is, crime and delinquency are still concentrated in certain neighborhoods in most cities. Bursik and Grasmick (1993) argue that lower-class, transient, high-crime neighborhoods are unable to marshal the resources and support, either from within the neighborhood or from public officials, to address the crime problems. This situation is exacerbated when change and turnover in an area increase. The solution to various neighborhood problems is to identify indigenous leadership, tap what resources do exist, and build a neighborhood coalition that can promote change. This view is readily apparent in the efforts of federal, state, and local governments to promote partnerships and grassroots efforts to fight community problems.

Ecological explanations often lead to a serious misinterpretation of the crime problem, however. What is found about an area may be attributed to individuals, for example. When crime occurs in areas of low income, low education, and high density, it is not unusual for some persons to claim that uneducated poor individuals from large families are criminal. This is not necessarily true. The offenders may fit this description or they may not. Using information about an area to make claims about individuals is called the *ecological fallacy*. In short, knowledge of an area says nothing about a specific individual.

It is interesting that some of the earliest attempts to address crime in neighborhoods and the community were the direct outcome of the work of Shaw and McKay. The Chicago Area Project, which began in 1931, attempted to mobilize the residents of high-crime neighborhoods as a direct attack on the problem of social disorganization. The project still exists in Chicago with the same basic goal of combating social problems at the grassroots level. This same idea is at the core of many of today's crime prevention activities, particularly neighborhood watch programs, the federal government's Project Weed and Seed, and community-oriented policing.

Sociological Learning Theories

Although the Chicago School is most often associated with the ecological perspective, the work of researchers in Chicago also developed a number of alternative theories for behavior, all from looking at the same situations as did Shaw and McKay. One of the more prominent learning theories is Sutherland's (1939) *differential association theory,* whose basic premise is that all behavior is learned through interactions with significant others. The degree to which an individual will be deviant is determined by contact with both conventional and deviant associations. An individual who has more contact with those advocating or condoning deviant and antisocial behavior will more likely engage in that behavior. According to Sutherland, the major sources of input in learning are parents and peers. Not all associations, however, have an equal influence on an individual. Rather, the associations vary along a number of dimensions that reflect the importance of the association to an individual, how long the parties have been associated, how often they have contact, and how long each contact lasts.

A key shortcoming in Sutherland's theory was that he discounted anything but face-to-face interactions. In no place in his discussion did he leave room for the influence of other inputs, such as the mass media. This is understandable given the fact that Sutherland did his work in the 1930s when the mass media was still in its infancy. The development of television and its proliferation in the 1950s prompted the expansion of learning theories to include the influence of real and fictional portrayals of individuals in the media. Glaser's (1956) *differential identification* theory argued that face-to-face interaction was not necessary for learning. Instead, juveniles could learn from characters they had seen in the mass media. Children also could assume the roles that they viewed on television or in the movies. Glaser simply added the influence of the mass media to Sutherland's ideas.

Other authors modified sociological learning theories to include the basic ideas of operant conditioning from psychology. Jeffery (1965) argued that individuals also learned from the consequences of their actions, an idea he termed *differential reinforcement.* Both social and nonsocial factors influence a person's behavior. For example, an individual who steals from a store may receive reinforcement either from the fact that the stolen food provides sustenance or from the accolades he receives from friends for getting away with it. The opposite is also true. Getting caught or being condemned for an action provides negative feedback and serves to mitigate future acts. Contemporary learning theory, therefore, argues that people receive a wide array of inputs, such as those from other people, the media, and nonsocial reinforcements and punishments.

The impact of learning theory can be seen in a wide array of social programs, both inside and outside the criminal justice system. One reason for this is the fact that the basic tenets of learning theory "just make sense." Detached worker programs can be viewed as a response to the ideas of learning theory. These programs place workers into gang settings to help direct their activity and provide nondeviant input to the decision making of the gangs and their members. Mentoring programs that pair nondeviant adults with at-risk kids in order to provide the youths with a positive role model also rest on the principles of learning theories. Finally, the growing recognition that media portrayals can influence the behavior of youths (i.e., learning theory) has led to the development of rating systems for movies, television, and music. These are only a few examples of sociologically oriented learning theory in action.

Subcultural Approaches

A third theoretical perspective stemming from the Chicago School tradition involves the idea that people may act in accordance with subcultural dictates, rather than the proscriptions of the larger society. The biggest challenge in subcultural explanations is in defining a subculture. Most definitions of a *subculture* include a reference to a set of values, beliefs, ideas, views, or a combination of these that differ from those of the larger culture. This does not mean that the subculture is totally different. By definition, a subculture operates within the larger culture and, to some extent, relies on some of the values, beliefs, and views of the larger culture.

Subcultural theories of crime view antisocial behavior as an unintended consequence of people attempting to follow the dictates of the subculture. The intent is not to break the laws of the larger culture. Law violation is simply a consequence of abiding by subcultural values and beliefs. People may turn to subcultures because they feel they do not fit into the larger culture or they are unsuccessful at operating by larger cultural dictates. They may also have been taught or have learned the subcultural values and beliefs more than those of the larger culture, or they simply may not realize that their actions conform to one group and not another.

The early subcultural theories focused on the behavior of lower-class individuals. Cohen (1955) recognized that delinquency was concentrated among lower-class boys and argued that those youths could not compete successfully in a middle-class society. The failure that accompanied attempts to adhere to middle-class values and beliefs led to feelings of inadequacy and poor self-image. Consequently, the youths turned to others in a similar situation and established a new set of reference points for their behavior: a gang subculture. Acting in accordance with the subcultural mandates provided the youths with a sense of accomplishment, increased feelings of self-worth, and status. At the same time, it invariably resulted in conflict with middle-class society. This culture conflict meant that the youths would be labeled as deviant and sanctioned for their behavior. In describing the lower-class gang subculture, Cohen (1955) claimed that it revolved around being malicious, negativistic, and nonutilitarian.

Miller (1958) provided a second well-known attempt to discuss a lower-class subculture. Instead of focusing on juvenile gang behavior, Miller proposed that the lower class had a different set of *focal con-*

cerns, or values, than the dominant middle class. These focal concerns were trouble, toughness, smartness, excitement, fate, and autonomy. These concerns were indicative of a need for immediate, short-term gratification that could be best addressed through taking chances, being streetwise, and exerting one's independence from rules and regulations. Naturally, following these focal concerns would lead to violations of the law and being subjected to the dictates of the dominant culture.

Both Cohen's and Miller's arguments suffer from similar problems; namely, they look at the behavior of lower-class individuals and try to impute the values that underlie those actions. That is, they are assuming that these individuals have the values and beliefs that Cohen and Miller articulated, based solely on looking at what people do. In reality, values cannot be assumed by just looking at behavior. Compounding this problem is the fact that both Cohen and Miller were middle-class researchers who were looking at the behavior of lower-class individuals and making judgments from a middle-class orientation. Lower-class individuals may not see their behavior in the same way as did these researchers.

An important concern when discussing subcultures is recognizing that individuals in a subculture are also operating in the larger culture. Indeed, many individuals try to adhere to both the subcultural and cultural mandates at the same time. This has the potential of causing confusion for the individual. People acting in accordance with subcultural values may find ways to maintain their status in the larger culture and justify their deviant behavior. Sykes and Matza (1957) offered a set of *techniques of neutralization* that allow an individual to do just that. These techniques provide various ways to justify one's subcultural activities amid negative feedback from the larger culture. These techniques include the following: denial of responsibility (ultimate responsibility for the action lies elsewhere); denial of injury (nobody was really hurt); denial of victim (he had it coming); condemnation of the condemnors (those who condemn the individual are really no better); and appeal to higher loyalties (acting in accord with the more important group). Sykes and Matza argued that using these techniques allows an individual to operate simultaneously in both a subculture and the larger culture.

Subcultural arguments have not found their way into criminal justice and social practice as readily as some other theories. Certainly, subcultural arguments are useful for trying to understand the emergence of problems among different ethnic or racial groups, and for studying why some individuals become involved in deviant behaviors, while others do not. That information may be of value when trying to identify the proper way to approach people of different backgrounds who are either committing deviance or are in need of assistance. Indeed, this very thing occurs every day when attempting to mobilize neighborhoods, identify the proper treatment modality for offenders, and transplant programs into different locations. In some respects, efforts like these are paying heed to the basic tenets of subcultural theory, but the theory itself may not be the driving force in the activity.

Routine Activities and Rational Choice

The routine activities perspective also has ties to the Chicago School and the ecology of crime by looking at the movement of offenders and victims through space and how that influences the level of crime. At the most basic level, the *routine activities perspective* views the normal daily behavior of people as contributing to the time, place, and level of criminal activity. Cohen and Felson (1979) argued that in order for crime to occur, three things must coincide: a motivated offender, a suitable target, and the absence of guardians. They illustrated their argument by noting that the increase in household property crime since the 1950s corresponded with the advent of two-earner households (which left homes empty and unguarded during the day) and the availability of portable goods (increasingly smaller, more valuable belongings, such as electronic devices). This same type of finding has emerged in a number of other studies and is the argument underlying many crime prevention initiatives.

An important companion piece to routine activities is *rational choice theory*, which assumes that potential offenders make choices about when, where, and how to commit offenses (Cornish & Clarke, 1986). This would explain why many studies of crime prevention initiatives show that homeowners who take actions to make crimes (such as burglary) more difficult see a decrease in victimization, whereas area homeowners who do not take precautions do not see a change. Studies of burglars show that the offenders choose which homes to burglarize on the basis of a variety of cues (Lab, 2000). Rational choice does not mean that all crime is planned out, however. Many offenders undertake their activities when opportunities arise during the course of nondeviant pursuits. Hence, a choice is made about whether to commit the crime or to refrain. Not all theorists agree that offenders are rational, and some suggest that offenders focus mainly on the rewards to be gained while ignoring the risks. They view offenders as acting more on impulse than on any real, rational decision making.

The routine activities and rational choice perspectives have had a great deal of impact on efforts to fight crime. Many crime prevention activities, particularly situational crime prevention, which targets problems with individualized interventions, draw from these theories. Any action that attempts to increase the risk of getting caught while committing a crime (such as increased police patrol, the installation of alarms and cameras, and increasing the presence of other people) is implementing the underlying ideas of both routine activities and rational choice. Indeed, preventive action taken by the criminal justice system and society is in some way addressing at least part of these theories.

Social Control Theories

Social control theories are among the leading sociological explanations of behavior and take a unique approach to explaining deviant behavior. Rather than identifying factors that force an individual to violate the law, *social control* explanations look at factors that keep an individual from participating in criminal activity. This is a very important distinction because the absence of the control factors does not necessarily mean that the person will be deviant. Instead, their absence simply means that there is an increased chance of deviance. Control theories look at why people *do not* become deviant.

As envisioned by Hirschi (1969), delinquent acts result when an individual's bond to society is weak or broken. His assumption was that an individual's behavior is controlled by relationships and connections the person has with conventional society. The more a person is tied to parents, friends, school, work, religion, and other elements of society, the less likely the individual will engage in deviant activity. Deviance appears when the ties to conventional social order are destroyed or diminished and the person chooses to act in a deviant fashion. The key for Hirschi's social control is the idea of *bond to society*, which is a result of socialization during childhood. Hirschi (1969) outlined four elements of bond: attachment (caring about what others think); commitment (investing in conventional endeavors); involvement (spending time and energy on conventional activities); and belief (acceptance of the conventional value system). When individuals do not care about what other people think, do not strive for socially acceptable goals, do not get involved in conventional behaviors, do not accept the values and beliefs of the larger society, or a combination of these, there is an increased opportunity to engage in deviant behaviors. Although the chances for deviant behaviors are increased, there is no guarantee that they will appear.

Another variation of social control theory is Reckless' (1962) containment theory. The biggest difference between Hirschi's social control and Reckless' containment theory is that the former approach relies exclusively on controls that are imposed on the individual through early socialization and training by others, while *containment theory* suggests that the individual has some influence over his own behavior. Reckless offered two sources of control: inner and outer containment. Outer containment approximates elements of Hirschi's theory and includes things like social pressure, supervision, and the influence of family, peers, and the social environment. Inner containment reflects more individualized factors, such as tolerance of frustration, goal directedness, and a positive self-concept. Though the elements of inner containment may be influenced by other people, they are distinctly individualized. Beyond inner and outer containment, Reckless noted that a variety of other factors can play a role in determining behavior, such as poverty, inequality, restlessness, anxiety, and deviant peers. As is the case with social control theory, although these various factors make turning to deviant behavior easier, they do not cause the behavior.

An interesting variation on social control is Messner and Rosenfeld's (1997) discussion of how the focus on monetary success in the United States has led to the disintegration of informal social controls in society. The authors pointed out that society's disproportionate emphasis on monetary success fails to recognize that not everyone has the ability or means to be successful (see also the following discussion of strain theory). They argue that the family, schools, and other potential sources of control have become obsessively concerned with monetary success. At the same time, those institutions fail to socialize youths and provide the control necessary to keep youths from deviant behavior (Messner & Rosenfeld, 1997). Accordingly, what is needed is a devaluation of economic success and a renewed emphasis on the proper socialization of youths.

The most recent variation on control theory suggests that controls do not have to persist throughout the life of an individual. Gottfredson and Hirschi (1990) proposed a *self-control theory* that suggests that self-control, internalized early in life, can keep a person from violating the law throughout the life span. This differs from Hirschi's earlier social control theory, in that the former explanation assumed that the bond to society had to persist throughout a person's life (i.e., in the form of attachments, commitment, involvement, and beliefs) to keep a person from deviance. Self-control suggests that the early socialization can be sufficient for reining in any later temptation to break the law. Gottfredson and Hirschi assumed that humans are hedonistic and make choices based solely on the pleasure that can be gained. Self-control allows the individual to refrain from acting on those hedonistic desires. Since the primary source of self-control is good parenting, the theory argues that the best time to intervene is in very early childhood. Self-control must be internalized early. If the parents fail to teach good self-control at home, it may be too late to effectively change behavior once the youth enters school or other social situations.

The ideas of social control underlie many initiatives for dealing with problem youths. Efforts to establish programs that involve youths in different activities and pro-social groups, to train families and schools to properly socialize the children under their care, and to help families to build strong ties between parents and offspring, all address the basic tenets of social control and self-control theory. As with learning theories, the fact that control theory is easily understood means it finds a great deal of acceptance among members of the criminal justice system and social policy makers.

Strain Theories

Strain theory shifts the emphasis from the individual and views deviance as a direct result of the social structure. The makeup and form of society thus dictate that some people will break the law because society is unable to provide equal opportunities for success to every individual. Modern society is composed of specialized jobs that bring different rewards, and some individuals will necessarily receive more for their contributions than others. At the same time, man is considered to be egoistic, which means that he aspires to achieve, get as much as the next guy, and realize his expectations. The inability of egoistic individuals to realize their expectations creates a condition known as anomie (Durkheim, 1933). Loosely translated, *anomie* refers to a state of normlessness or inadequate regulation. It is the inability of individuals to recognize that they cannot get every- thing they want given the limitations of society. One's desires simply do not match up with the available opportunities. Because egoistic individuals cannot regulate their own desires, it is therefore incum- bent on society to place restrictions on them.

The basic ideas of anomie and the disjuncture between desired goals and available means to those goals form the foundation of strain theory. Merton (1938) argued that the strain individuals feel between goals and means leads to deviant behavior. Specifically, he identified five different *modes of adaptation,* or ways that individuals may respond to the strain between goals and means. Most people respond with *conformity* and simply do their best to achieve the goals through socially prescribed means. *Innovation* occurs when people accept socially prescribed goals, but find innovative (unacceptable) means to achieve the goals. Individuals who give up on the goals, but continue to act in socially acceptable ways even though they know they will not succeed, fall into the *ritualism* mode. *Retreatism* reflects a total denial of both the socially prescribed goals and the legitimate means to achieve these goals. A prime example of this is the case of an individ- ual who uses and abuses drugs. The final mode of adaptation is *rebel- lion,* in which individuals attempt to change both the accepted goals and the means of society. The adaptation that is used depends on the circumstances and background of each individual (Merton, 1938).

The largest criticism of strain theory has been that not everyone feels strain from the inability to achieve society's goals. Agnew (1992) proposed a *general strain theory* that argues that strain can come from other sources. One source of strain can be the removal of desired stimuli, such as restricting someone's activities. A second source may be the introduction of negative stimuli that may cause anger or frus- tration, such as being harassed at work or school. These sources of strain can prompt individuals to strike out against society and others who are perceived as causing the strain (Agnew, 1992). Both general strain theory and traditional strain theory suggest that the solution to crime is to address the social structure that places individuals into some form of stressful situation.

Strain theory has had a major impact since the mid-1960s. In the midst of social turmoil in the United States, President Johnson initiated a wide array of social reforms that have come to be known as the Great Society reforms. Included among these was the implementation of Head Start programs for preschool youths, job training programs for adults, an emphasis on improving educational achievement, and the creation of new jobs. All of these efforts were a direct result of the recognition that many individuals, particularly racial and ethnic minorities, were ill-prepared to succeed in society. Further, there were limited chances to succeed (i.e., good jobs) even if they were prepared. Many programs today address the same problems of individuals wanting to succeed.

The Labeling Perspective

The labeling perspective also places the blame for much deviance on society. *Labeling* argues that by processing individuals through formal mechanisms of social control, society labels the individuals as deviant and forces them to think of themselves as deviant. The consequences of labeling are actions by individuals in accordance to their labels. That is, if an individual sees himself as a criminal, he will commit crime.

An important concept underlying labeling is the idea of *symbolic interactionism,* which claims that individuals develop their self-image through interaction with other people (Mead, 1934). Basically, a person's self-image reflects what he thinks others perceive when they look at him. The self-image is then actualized in the behavior of the individual.

The leading proponent of the labeling perspective, Edwin Lemert, distinguished between two different types of deviance. *Primary deviance* entails activities that are viewed as a normal part of living in society and are not perceived as central to the identity of individuals (Lemert, 1951). This type of deviance does not lead to negative labels that are applied to people. On the other hand, *secondary deviance* comprises deviant acts that occur as a result of individuals acting in accordance with being labeled. That is, an individual has been labeled as a deviant and decides to commit deviant acts because that is who he believes he is. The only difference between primary and secondary deviance is the reason behind the act. If it is a result of a person being labeled, it is secondary deviance. If it is rationalized as a part of normal social activity, it is primary deviance. There is no difference in the type of crime, only in how the actor views himself. One solution to reducing the level of crime, therefore, is to limit the degree of labeling that takes place. Because participation in the criminal and juvenile justice systems is viewed as a major venue for labeling, keeping people out of the system should cut back on the application of labels and, thus, the level of crime.

The labeling perspective had a huge impact on the operations of the juvenile justice system. It was one of the major theories used in the 1967 President's Commission on Law Enforcement and Administration of Justice Task Force Report, "Juvenile Delinquency and Youth Crime." The commission recognized that the system was overcrowded and that system intervention was causing more problems than it was solving. They recommended that the system should attempt to remove youths from the system and keep them out of formal processing as much as possible. The result was a strong movement in the criminal justice system toward deinstitutionalizing status offenders (see the discussion in Chapter 6) and other minor offenders by using more community-based interventions and simply ignoring much minor juvenile misbehavior. Many of those efforts persist today and can be seen in the use of informal, rather than formal, probation; the development of community correctional programs; and federal mandates to keep status offenders out of secure facilities.

Conflict Theories

Conflict theories provide the most direct link between social structure and deviant behavior. Where the previous sociological theories take law as a given and assume that the existing structure of society is appropriate, conflict theory raises questions about the making and breaking of laws and the appropriate form of society. At the most basic level, *conflict theories* argue that the making and enforcement of laws are an outcome of competition among different groups in society, rather than the result of consensus over what should be criminalized. The group that has the power and resources to win the conflict is able to pass laws that criminalize the behavior or activities of other groups. Conflict arguments generally fall into two camps, pluralistic and radical. *Pluralistic conflict* takes the position that many different interest groups attempt to influence public policy. Different groups will wield the most power in a conflict depending on the issue and the support they can garner (Turk, 1980). Conversely, *radical conflict* (also known as critical or Marxist conflict) sees the existence of only two groups, the "haves" and the "have nots." The "haves," by virtue of their economic position, hold the power in any conflict and can always dictate what and who is considered criminal. The decision invariably falls along economic lines. This does not mean that the "have nots" never get things they want. They get them, however, only when the "haves" decide to let them prevail or when it is seen as in their own interest as well. Under both types of conflict, crime is a result of one group's actions being criminalized by the group with power.

Beyond discussions of how law is constructed, the more radical forms of conflict theory argue that the form of society is a major source of deviant behavior. Capitalism, which restricts the accumulation of wealth to a small segment of the population, creates a social structure that generates crime. As more and more wealth is held by an ever smaller group and an increasingly larger proportion of the population is marginalized and made to work for a diminishing level of return, many individuals will strike out against society. Radical conflict sees the law as maintaining the status quo by criminalizing the behavior of those who are potential threats to capitalism. The law and its agents' behavior are viewed as mechanisms by which the existing inequalities in society are maintained. According to conflict theory, the solution to crime is to alter the form of society so that every individual has an equal opportunity to succeed.

An extension of conflict theory is feminist theory. At their inception, *feminist theories* critiqued the existing criminological theories because they focused primarily on male deviance and misrepresented female deviant behavior. Today, feminist theories explore the differences between male and female criminality by focusing on perceived gender, class, and racial inequalities in the social system.

Conflict theories have had little effect on the operations of the criminal justice system. In the broadest sense, these theories suggest major changes in the structure of society and law. Any changes in the criminal justice system would have a minimal impact if larger social changes were not also made. This situation is endemic to the view that the criminal justice system is a tool of the dominant group or class in society. Most use of conflict theory appears in historical reinterpretations of the development of the criminal justice system and why the system does what it does. A good example of this is Platt's (1977) analysis of the development of the juvenile court, where he argued that the court was established by the upper classes as a mechanism for controlling the lower classes and further solidifying the ruling class's position of power. This does not mean that conflict theories have had no impact. Feminist theories and arguments have made some progress in altering the way the criminal justice system responds to and handles female offenders and victims, for example. Such changes may be evident, but the overriding problem of how society can be restructured has not been addressed.

Theory Integration

The failure of any one theory to explain criminal and deviant behavior adequately has led some writers to propose the integration of different theories into more unified, coherent explanations. These endeavors are variously referred to as theory *integration,* the *elaboration model,* and *life course approaches.* Basically, parts of different theories are brought together into what may be a better explanation of criminal behavior. Elliott and his colleagues (1985) have attempted to build a model that incorporates parts of social control, strain, and differential association theories. In recent years, a growing interest in developmental theories suggests different causal mechanisms at work at different points in the life span. Life course studies look at different influences on behavior at different points in life (Moffitt, 1997).

The following possibility of theory integration serves as an example. Biological factors during prenatal development may result in learning disabilities that come into play later in a person's life. Upon reaching school age, a youth may struggle to learn and succeed academically, which can lead one to being singled out as different from other youths. This could lead to dropping out and eventually to having greater contact with deviant youths and thus delinquent activity. The lack of an education can result in poor job possibilities and the inability to succeed at legitimate endeavors. As the individual faces greater strains to succeed, deviance may be a preferable mode of activity. Throughout this example, biological, learning, social control, and strain theories are readily apparent at different points in the individual's life. A variety of elaboration or integrative models has been proposed and tested, and this type of theory development appears to be the wave of the future in criminological theory.

Summary

Though theory is not typically discussed by those working in the criminal justice system, theories are important underlying factors for everything that occurs. As noted in this chapter, theory is simply an attempt to explain why something happens. Certainly, the changes that occur every day in the operations of the criminal justice system are not made in a vacuum. The changes are due to someone's belief about why things are happening and what will take place as a result of a new program, policy, law, or activity. Theory, therefore, is happening all around the criminal justice system. Despite this fact, it is increasingly important to be able to articulate theoretical explanations to justify the changes being proposed. This becomes much easier when there is a sense of what theories already exist, the arguments underlying those theories, and what to expect if changes are made on the basis of those theories.

References

Agnew, R. (1992). Foundation for a general strain theory of crime and delinquency. *Criminology, 30*(1), 47–87.

Bandura, A., & Walters, R. H. (1963). *Social learning and personality development.* New York: Holt, Rinehart and Winston.

Booth, A., & Osgood, D. W. (1993). The influence of testosterone on deviance in adulthood: Assessing and explaining the relationship. *Criminology, 31* (1), 93–118.

Bursik, R. J., & Grasmick, H. G. (1993). *Neighborhoods and crime: The dimensions of effective community control.* New York: Lexington.

Cohen, A. K. (1955). *Delinquent boys: The culture of the gang.* Glencoe, IL: Free Press.

Cohen, L. E., & Felson, M. (1979). Social changes and crime rate trends: A routine activities approach. *American Sociological Review, 44*(3), 588–608.

Cornish, D. B., & Clarke, R. V. (1986). *The reasoning criminal.* New York: Springer-Verlag.

Dalton, K. (1964). *The premenstrual syndrome.* Springfield, IL: Thomas.

Durkheim, E. (1933). *The division of labor in society.* (G. Supson, Trans.). New York: Free Press.

Elliott, D. S., Huizinga, D., & Ageton, S. S. (1985). *Explaining delinquency and drug use.* Beverly Hills, CA: Sage.

Glaser, D. (1956). Criminality theories and behavioral images. *American Journal of Sociology, 61*(2), 433–444.

Glueck, S., & Glueck, E. (1950). *Unraveling juvenile delinquency.* Cambridge, MA: Harvard University Press.

Glueck, S., & Glueck, E. (1956). *Physique and delinquency.* New York: Harper.

Gottfredson, M. R., & Hirschi, T. (1990). *A general theory of crime.* Stanford, CA: Stanford University Press.

Gray, G. E., & Gray, L. K. (1983). Diet and juvenile delinquency. *Nutrition Today, 18,* 14–21.

Hirschi, T. (1969). *Causes of delinquency.* Berkeley: University of California Press.

Jeffery, C. R. (1965). Criminal behavior and learning theory. *Journal of Criminal Law, Criminology, and Police Science, 56*(3), 294–300.

Kohlberg, L. (1981). *The philosophy of moral development.* San Francisco: Harper and Row.

Lab, S. P. (2000). *Crime prevention: Approaches, practices, and evaluations* (4th ed.). Cincinnati, OH: Anderson.

Lemert, E. M. (1951). *Social pathology: A systematic approach to the theory of sociopathic behavior.* New York: McGraw-Hill.

Lombroso, C. (1876). *On criminal man.* Milan, Italy: Hoepli.

Mead, G. H. (1934). *Mind, self, and society.* Chicago: University of Chicago Press.

Megargee, E. I., & Bohn, M. J. (1979). *Classifying criminal offenders: A new system based on the MMPI.* Beverly Hills, CA: Sage.

Merton, R. K. (1938). Social structure and anomie. *American Sociological Review, 3,* 672–682.

Messner, S. F., & Rosenfeld, R. (1997). *Crime and the American dream* (2nd ed.). Belmont, CA: Wadsworth.

Miller, W. B. (1958). Lower-class culture as a generating milieu of gang delinquency. *Journal of Social Issues, 15*(1), 5–19.

Moffitt, T. E. (1997). Adolescence-limited and life-course-persistent offending: A complementary pair of developmental theories. In T. P. Thornberry (Ed.), *Developmental theories of crime and delinquency.* New Brunswick, NJ: Transaction.

Platt, A. M. (1977). *The child savers: The invention of delinquency.* Chicago: University of Chicago Press.

Raine, A. (1993). *The psychopathology of crime.* San Diego, CA: Academic Press.

Reckless, W. C. (1962). A non-causal explanation: Containment theory. *Excerpta Criminologica, 1,* 131–134.

Reiss, A. J., & Roth, J. A. (1993). *Understanding and preventing violence* (Vol. 1). Washington, DC: National Academy Press.

Shaw, C. R., & McKay, H. D. (1942). *Juvenile delinquency and urban areas.* Chicago: University of Chicago Press.

Sheldon, W. H. (1949). *Varieties of delinquent youth: An introduction to correctional psychiatry.* New York: Harper and Brothers.

Skinner, B. F. (1953). *Science and human behavior.* New York: Macmillan.

Sullivan, C., Grant, M. Q., & Grant, J. D. (1957). The development of interpersonal maturity: Applications to delinquency. *Psychiatry, 20*(3), 373–385.

Sutherland, E. H. (1939). *Principles of criminology* (3rd ed.). Philadelphia: Lippincott.

Sykes, G. M., & Matza, D. (1957). Techniques of neutralization: A theory of delinquency. *American Sociological Review, 22*(3), 664–670.

Turk, A. T. (1980). Analyzing official deviance: For nonpartison conflict analysis in criminology. In J.A. Inciardi (Ed.), *Radical criminology: The coming crisis* (pp. 78–91). Beverly Hills, CA: Sage.

Van Voorhis, P., Braswell, M., & Lester, D. (1997). *Correctional counseling and rehabilitation* (3rd ed.). Cincinnati, OH: Anderson.

Suggested Readings

Bohm, R. M. (2001). *A primer on crime and delinquency theory* (2nd ed.). Belmont, CA: Wadsworth.

Cullen, F. T., & Agnew, R. (1999). *Criminological theory: Past to present: Essential readings.* Los Angeles: Roxbury Publishing.

LaFree, G. (Ed.). (2000). *The nature of crime: Continuity and change* (Criminal Justice 2000, Vol. 1). Washington, DC: National Institute of Justice.

Lynch, M. J., Michalowski, R. J., & Groves, W. B. (2000). *The new primer in radical criminology: Critical perspectives on crime, power, and identity.* Monsey, NY: Criminal Justice Press.

Messner, S. F., Krohn, M. D., & Liska, A. (1989). *Theoretical integration in the study of deviance and crime: Problems and prospects.* Albany, NY: SUNY Press.

Vold, G. B., Bernard, T. J., & Snipes, J. B. (2002). *Theoretical criminology* (5th ed.). New York: Oxford University Press.

Discussion Questions

1. Do you think that a general theory of crime that seeks to explain all (or most) criminal behavior is appropriate? Why or why not? What, if any, type of criminal behavior may require a unique theory and why?

2. Identify a particular criminal justice practice and discuss what theories, if any, most likely support that practice. Are there other theories of crime that suggest that such a practice may be ineffective or counterproductive? ✦

Chapter Three

Policing and Law Enforcement

Key Concepts and Terms

- Blue Wall of Silence
- Community Policing
- Discretion
- Homeland Security
- Law Enforcement
- Order Maintenance
- Police Subculture
- Problem-Oriented Policing
- Professionalism
- Use of Force
- Zero Tolerance

Introduction

As the law reflects the collective will of a people, the police are the "muscle" behind society's law. Those who do not voluntarily obey the law will have it imposed upon them; the police are the primary means by which the law is imposed. Although the police are thought of as *law enforcers,* arresting criminals is only a small portion of police work. The police also foster law compliance and provide an array of services that are not linked to crime. Almost 80 percent of a patrol officer's time is devoted to activities that are focused on other things, besides law enforcement.

In 1970, Egon Bittner described the role of the police "as a mechanism for the distribution of non-negotiably coercive force employed in accordance with the dictates of an intuitive grasp of situational exigencies" (Bittner, 1970, p. 46). The police may use force to insure that the law is obeyed and public order preserved. When the police actually use force is the essence of *police discretion.* It is not possible to write a law, or a rule, that will cover every possible situation the police might encounter. Nor will the police necessarily know with certainty every factual matter that attends every call they answer. The police combine their knowledge with the array of verbal and nonverbal information that attends each unique situation, make an accurate judgment about what is going on (the "situational exigencies"), and decide upon the proper response.

Not every police action is a coercive one, of course. The right to use force on behalf of society lies behind many of the other things police do. In broad terms, there are three primary responsibilities of police work: law enforcement, order maintenance, and service. These aspects were first explored by James Q. Wilson in his 1968 book, *Varieties of Police Behavior.*

Law Enforcement

"Enforcing the law" by apprehending criminals after crimes occur is an important part of police work, but it is only one element of the law enforcement mission. The entertainment media portray policing as an exciting career of criminal hunting, thwarting robberies in progress, engaging in high-speed car chases, making dynamic entries, and apprehending desperate criminals. In truth, these events happen infrequently. Far more than confronting so-called "master criminals," the police are likely to deal with crimes committed by people who are drunk, depressed, mentally ill, or simply overwhelmed by life stresses.

Tense confrontations, take-down moves, and an enticing array of high-tech weaponry and science seem to be the tools of the trade. But far more important tools are patience, good communication skills, and knowledge of human psychology. The ability to enforce the law by bringing criminals to justice rests in large part on the willingness of the public to cooperate with the police. The foundation for that is laid in the routine interaction between police and citizens in the course of everyday, nonemergency activities.

Crime prevention has been a prime function of police work, ensuring the safety of the community by denying criminals the opportunity to commit crime and defusing volatile situations before they reach the point of violence. Visible patrol-on foot, in motor vehicles, or on horseback-is seen as a means of preventing crime by *deterrence* of wrongdoers. Active patrol raises the possibility that a criminal will be seen and apprehended. The impression that the police are always around, and ever-vigilant, discourages criminals from committing crime. Often, the presence of authority, backed up by powers of arrest, will scatter potential troublemakers or quiet boisterous behavior. Gang intelligence helps defuse feuds that otherwise might turn violent, and skilled officers sometimes negotiate truces between rival gangs.

Police foster crime prevention in other, less flashy ways as well. Officers help organize and support community-based self-help activities, like *Neighborhood Watch,* to observe and report suspicious activity in the neighborhood. Community involvement may range from supplemental citizen patrols to initiating court action against landlords of properties where drug sales take place.

Patrol officers, school resource officers (SROs), Police Activity League (PAL) volunteers, and others participate in a wide variety of community-building activities, both on- and off-duty, to keep youngsters safe and to encourage law-abiding activities. Officers host self-defense workshops and conduct property surveys to help reduce individuals' risks of victimization, and they make numerous referrals to social service agencies across a wide spectrum of problems.

Order Maintenance

Crime is not the only thing in modern life that can cause concern. All sorts of conflicts can cause alarm, fear, or inconvenience. Loud and boisterous groups of teenagers, heated, chest-thumping bar arguments, and noisy arguments over finances between a husband and wife in the next apartment all disturb the peace and tranquility of neighbors. The police are called to these and many other situations not so much to make an arrest as to restore order. Though arrests are possible, most incidents are resolved through other means: mediation, referral, or the mere threat of arrest. In some cases, such as a dispute between a landlord and tenant over the payment of the rent, the police may have no legal authority in the matter (rent disputes are a matter of civil law), but they may serve as a referee. Their presence and authority act as a safety valve: both parties can back down without losing face.

Service

Service, the third function of the police, takes a wide variety of forms depending upon the location. Directions, assistance to disabled motorists, funeral escorts, administration of various kinds of permits, emergency relays of blood, checking vacant residences or looking in on vulnerable adults, aiding with traffic control at road construction and emergency scenes, and many more services are provided by local police and sheriff's deputies.

Because of this wide diversity of tasks, police officers are trained to be generalists. Most officers begin their careers doing uniformed patrol work. They will be called upon to answer an almost unimaginable array of different needs. Among these include assisting in childbirth, breaking up fights, talking down suicidal "jumpers," interviewing abused children, trading gunfire with desperate criminals, intervening in domestic arguments, assisting mentally ill and confused persons, and investigating corrupt police officers.

Police officers frequently describe their work as "long hours of sheer boredom, punctuated by moments of sheer terror." In contrast to Hollywood portrayals, the reality of police work is that exciting events happen infrequently and favorable results can be elusive. Those who expect exciting careers in law enforcement are likely to find that much of their time is devoted to social work, helping people cope with life, occasionally resolving low-level problems, and building interpersonal relationships with the community.

Structure

Police agencies have different mandates depending upon their level of political authority, region of the country, or specific charter of the agency. Government police agencies are authorized at the local, tribal, county, state, and federal levels. In addition, various special police forces may be authorized.

Local

The blue uniforms and patrol cars of the nation's municipal police forces provide the image most associated with the police. Their legal jurisdiction is usually limited to the borders of the town or city that hires them, though there are exceptions. Fresh pursuit of a suspect, mutual aid compacts among municipalities, and being sworn in as special officers or deputies for other agencies all may extend police officers' local authority.

Most municipal police agencies are small. Uniformed generalist patrol work is a universal entry point, and many officers spend most of their career doing patrol work. In larger departments, increased specialization in the form of detective, juvenile officer, SWAT team member, and so forth is possible in later career steps, as are promotions to supervisory positions.

Sheriff

The county sheriff is one of the oldest police offices and in many states is authorized by the state constitution. Unique among law enforcement, sheriffs serve all three branches of criminal justice: policing, courts (sheriffs provide security to courtrooms and serve civil and criminal writs), and corrections (sheriffs run most county jails). Deputy sheriffs often start their careers in the jail as correctional officers and work their way up to uniformed patrol and investigations.

Sheriffs are elected officials in 48 of the 50 states, but the duties of sheriff's departments vary regionally. In the South and West, sheriffs provide the primary law enforcement for many rural and unincorporated areas. In the urban centers of the Northeast, they tend to be court officers, but they provide only limited law enforcement because most of their jurisdiction has full-time municipal police.

In some of the densely populated urban areas, county police departments have taken over the law enforcement duties of the sheriff. Organized like large municipal departments, county departments are responsible to the county executive or county council rather than to an elected sheriff. County police may have concurrent jurisdiction with municipal police agencies located within the county. In such instances, like the sheriff's offices and state police, the county police tend to concentrate on areas without other police resources, cooperating with the municipal departments when the need arises.

Special Police

State laws authorize police forces for special limited purposes, such as to serve railroads (which run through multiple jurisdictions), college campuses, school districts, mass transit systems, parks and woodlands, and the like. The best known is the Port Authority of New York and New Jersey Police, which lost many officers in the September 11, 2001, attack on the World Trade Center.

A variation on the special police concept is the use of part-time officers (variously called "reserves," "special officers," or "auxiliary officers," among other titles) who work for municipal, county, and sheriff's departments in addition to their regular jobs. They may work either on an hourly paid basis or as unpaid volunteers, depending upon the agency and the state's authorizing statutes. With proper training, they may perform full police duties, especially in rural areas. Otherwise, they supplement regular police in support roles: directing traffic, crowd control at major events like concerts and fairs, and assisting in a variety of roles. Many sheriff's departments have "sheriff's posses" who can be called upon for additional staffing of special events and search-and-rescue operations. Their powers usually are less than those of full-time officers, but they provide valuable resources and expertise.

State

State police functions take one of two forms. State police have general law enforcement duties and general jurisdiction throughout the state. State patrols or highway patrols primarily enforce traffic laws on state highways; they have police powers and training, but no general police jurisdiction. States with highway patrols may also have an independent bureau of criminal investigation that provides criminal investigation and crime lab services across the state. Other elements of state government may employ investigators and officers with special police powers, such as the welfare, motor vehicle, revenue, alcoholic beverage control, and natural resources departments.

Some jurisdictions grant police powers to corrections employees, especially probation and parole officers.

Federal

Federal agencies have specific powers and jurisdiction under federal law and do not enforce state or local laws. There are more than 80 federal law enforcement agencies, including the Border Patrol, Customs Service, Federal Protective Services, U.S. Mint Police, and smaller police forces for various parts of the federal government (Capitol, Supreme Court, Environmental Protection Agency, etc.). Some crimes, such as bank robbery, are found in both state and federal statutes, leading to concurrent or overlapping jurisdiction.

Created in 1908, the Federal Bureau of Investigation (FBI) has a mandate to investigate approximately 200 federal crimes, including bank robbery and kidnapping, unless Congress specifically designates jurisdiction to another agency. Criminal acts and conspiracies that cross state lines usually fall to the FBI, the enforcement arm of the Justice Department. The FBI crime lab provides forensic support for investigators throughout the nation, and the National Academy provides advanced training for state and local officers. Recognizing the emerging needs created by globalization, the FBI has established offices in foreign countries and has been involved in the training of police forces in emerging nations and the countries of the former Soviet bloc.

The Drug Enforcement Administration (DEA) was established in 1973, combining several existing antidrug offices under the Justice Department. The DEA has primary responsibility for coordinating national drug enforcement efforts and is the sole agency authorized to pursue overseas drug investigations.

The Bureau of Alcohol, Tobacco, and Firearms (ATF or BATF) is an enforcement arm of the Treasury Department. Created in 1972 when it was split from the Internal Revenue Service, ATF has powers based in the tax laws and other federal laws and regulations relating to alcohol, tobacco products, firearms, explosives, and arson. Another Treasury function, the Secret Service, was created in 1865 to investigate money counterfeiting. Protection of the President of the United States was added after the 1901 assassination of President McKinley. Fraud in commerce and fictitious securities documents are also within its investigative mandate.

The U.S. Marshals Service is the oldest federal law enforcement agency, created by the Judiciary Act of 1789. Marshals protect the federal judiciary, transport federal prisoners, and protect endangered federal witnesses (the Witness Protection Program). In addition, marshals manage assets seized from criminal enterprises.

Tribal

The U.S. Constitution recognizes Indian tribes as sovereign entities, and tribal lands may have their own police forces. The federal Bureau of Indian Affairs (BIA) also has a separate police force for tribal lands, whose territorial dimensions may cross municipal, county, and even state lines.

Homeland Security

At the time of this writing, federal law enforcement is undergoing a dramatic restructuring. As a response to the September 11, 2001, terrorist attacks on the World Trade Center and the Pentagon, President George W. Bush and Congress created the Department of Homeland Security. Its primary missions are to "protect America from future terrorist attacks, reduce America's vulnerability to terrorism, and minimize the damage and recover from" such attacks as may occur (*http://www.whitehouse.gov/deptofhomeland/sect2.html*). The four divisions of the department will be "border and transportation security; emergency preparedness and response; countermeasures for chemical, biological, radiological, and nuclear events; and information analysis and infrastructure protection" (*http://www.whitehouse.gov/deptofhomeland/sect2.html*). Several federal law-enforcement agencies, including the Customs Service, the coast Guard, the Immigration and Naturalization Service, and the Border Patrol, will be incorporated under Homeland Security, along with the Animal and Plant Health Inspection Service, the Transportation Security Administration, and the Federal Emergency Management Administration (FEMA). Homeland Security will also bear the responsibility for coordinating the intelligence-gathering and analysis functions of the FBI, CIA, and National Security Agency, along with the executive protection functions of the Treasury Department's Secret Service.

Organization

Sworn officers in American police and law enforcement agencies are organized in a hierarchical form, with a *chain of command* conveying information from the line to the administrative decision makers and conveying orders and information back down. In larger departments, patrol officers report to shift supervisors (sergeants), who report to shift commanders (lieutenants), who report to precinct commanders (captains). Precinct and unit commanders report to divisional heads (deputy chiefs). Police work is organized by task requirements (sworn or civilian) as well as by geography and by time.

Sworn vs. Civilian

For many years, almost every position in a police department was held by a uniformed police officer or a plainclothes detective. Women held only secretarial jobs and "matron" positions in jails. Support positions could be places to which officers were assigned as a punitive measure or the "plum jobs" that offered a daytime Monday to Friday refuge from rotating shift work.

In modern times, many departments employ civilians (also called non-sworn or contract employees) to perform tasks that do not require the extensive police training and experience of a sworn officer. Records, dispatching, fleet maintenance, personnel and budget, and even crime scene investigations may be staffed by non-sworn personnel. They are trained only for their special function, do not have police powers or carry weapons, and generally are paid much less than sworn officers.

Patrol officers have general duties, attending to a wide variety of calls and situations. In order for police departments to function efficiently, however, a number of specialist duties must be filled. Best known is the work of the detectives or investigators, who do not answer calls. Their time is spent interviewing witnesses and following up on leads in unsolved crime cases. Detectives may specialize in a certain type of crime (homicide, burglary, robbery, sex crimes, etc.) or conduct all kinds of criminal investigation. Crime analysis, gang intelligence and intervention, school resource officers, training coordinator, HAZMAT (hazardous material), and high-risk warrant service, among others, are task-specific functions for sworn officers.

Geography

In the smallest local departments, officers are responsible for covering the entire town or village. Elsewhere, officers work specific parts of town called *beats*. The officer is responsible for answering all calls within that beat as well as for preventing crimes and resolving problems.

Larger agencies are organized into *precincts* containing several beats. There are, for instance, seventy-six precincts in New York City, six in Austin, Texas, and four in Minneapolis, Minnesota. It is easier to manage smaller areas within a large city, enabling the precinct commander to be more responsive to citizen concerns.

Sheriff's departments may also divide into different districts or may operate out of a central office. In addition, sheriff's offices may assign deputies to local municipalities, known as *contract* cities, for a specified number of hours according to a contract negotiated between the city and the sheriff. Contracts guarantee basic police services while relieving smaller cities of part of the expense of maintaining their own departments.

The phrase *beat integrity* refers to a policy of keeping officers assigned to one specific beat consistently so they may develop knowledge about the players in and build relationships with the community. This represents a significant change from the pre-1960s policies that moved officers frequently to different areas of the city in an effort to thwart corruption. Nonetheless, officers may cross beat boundaries to assist other officers if necessary.

State police agencies must cover entire states and organize into *troops* for the same reasons that police departments organize into precincts. In rural areas, troopers may operate out of their homes (such as the Connecticut Resident Trooper program), but are responsible to a troop-level administration.

Federal agencies responsible for national coverage organize into administrative regions and generally maintain offices in major cities. Federal agencies also work cooperatively with local and state agencies through *regional task forces* for various purposes, recognizing that crime does not confine itself to jurisdictional boundaries. Short-term task forces may devote their efforts to tracking down a serial rapist or a prolific bank robber. Long-term resources are devoted to organized crime, such as racketeering, insurance fraud, illegal drug importation and distribution, and smuggling.

Time

Because crime and public emergencies occur around the clock, dispatch services and police coverage must be 24 hours a day, 7 days a week. Police agencies tend to staff their shifts differently according to the volume of activity expected for various parts of the day. There are many different shift schedules, ranging from the standard 40-hour work week of five 8-hour days, to the popular 4-10 and 3-12 shifts (four ten-hour or three twelve-hour days). The two basic models are *rotating shifts* in which officers periodically change from days to evenings to nights, and steady shifts in which work hours are determined by a seniority system or a bid lottery.

Overlapping shifts and power shifts provide extra police presence during the active evening hours and on weekends. Extra officers are available to handle the call load and provide backup in dangerous situations. Smaller agencies may provide nighttime coverage by an "on-call" arrangement. Officers work their shifts and return home to sleep, but they can be called out again for an accident or some criminal incident. Another agency, such as the sheriff's office or state police, also may provide after-hours coverage.

Investigators and crime scene technicians generally work day and evening shifts, with either minimum staffing or on-call status for the overnight hours. Other support positions, such as records, planning and research, personnel, purchase and supply, and so forth, usually do not work around the clock or on weekends. They tend to be Monday to Friday offices because their work entails interaction with other public and private sector offices on the standard work schedule.

Police Work and Career Paths

Municipal policing remains a single-point-of-entry career. Officers working in municipal departments begin in patrol, doing shift work and answering a wide variety of calls. The diversity of patrol activities provides a learning base of experience. After that, three basic career paths are possible: Officers may remain in patrol for their entire careers; they may move from patrol into some specialty role, most typically as an investigator or detective; or they may follow a mixed career of supervisory promotions and specialty assignments that lead to administrative posts.

Sheriff's departments may have single- or dual-entry tracks. *Single-entry tracks* mean that deputies begin their careers working in the jails, unarmed, supervising prisoners. When a patrol position becomes available, jail deputies have the first opportunity for the slot, subject to seniority and testing rules. The emerging professional movement in corrections has led some sheriffs to create *dual-entry tracks*. Deputies hired for the corrections functions are hired with an understanding that they will be working only in the jail, and persons seeking law enforcement positions apply directly for patrol positions. Jail deputies may apply for patrol slots later if they wish, but they do so on a level playing field, with no seniority advantages or "inside track" compared with outsiders.

The Hiring Process

The older police career model, which still endures in many areas, began with candidates being hired by an agency. At that point, the town or city sent them to a police academy for training and state certification as a police officer. As police training and education requirements expanded, other options developed. Today, persons seeking a police career may pay for their own *preservice training* before being hired, which may give them a competitive edge in the job market.

In some states, they can pay to go to a regular police academy. In others, alternative police certification processes are housed in academic programs at two-year community and vocational colleges. Students graduate with an associate's degree and state certification as a police officer, although they have no police powers until an agency hires them. Preservice certification represents a savings for the municipality, which can put the officer to work immediately and spare the municipality the cost of training.

Police recruits must pass a battery of tests to be hired, even with preservice certification. Written, psychological, and physical tests, as well as background checks for character and conduct, are standard in most areas. Some agencies require polygraph exams; still others will put candidates through an assessment center to test their skills and instinctive reactions in various situations.

Field Training

Most departments have a full-time *Field Training Officer (FTO)* program that provides the bridge between academy learning and autonomous authority in the field. Officers ride with more experienced officers who have a mandate to expose the rookies to as many situations as possible, evaluating and critiquing the trainees' responses as part of the field learning process. Once the FTO program is complete, the rookie may work independently, but most will undergo an additional period as probationary employees. If their performance is poor, they can be released without any further action. If they successfully pass their probationary period, they become full-fledged members of the agency and are accorded all civil service and bargaining unit protections where applicable.

Promotion

The requirements for being promoted to supervisory rank or to specialty positions vary widely. At the low end, seniority is still found in some departments. The person who has been in the department the longest gets the next open position, regardless of training, education, or general fitness for the job. At the other end of the spectrum are batteries of written tests, oral interviews, and assessment center tests. A few departments also incorporate a "promotability score" on the basis of past performance and supervisors' assessments of an individual's skills that will be necessary for the new job.

Specialties. Criminal investigation often requires a long-term commitment to cases, interviewing people, following up leads, assessing physical evidence, and preparing affidavits for warrants and cases for court. It is difficult to conduct investigations if one is always being called off to answer another call for service, so most police agencies have an investigative specialist position, usually called *detective*. In some agencies, detective is a rank and is considered a promotion above patrol officer. In others, it is considered an assignment and holds the same rank within the organization as a patrol officer.

Because of its high profile and clarity of focus, the job of criminal investigations, or detective work, is a prized assignment for many police officers. In smaller organizations, detectives are investigative generalists. In larger agencies, detectives are specialized, devoting their time to a single category of crime. They may work in several different investigative units over the course of their careers.

Undercover assignments are a special type of investigation, in which the officers pretend to be criminals or "fringe players" in order to gather intelligence on criminal networks or to buy drugs and stolen merchandise. Occasionally, undercover police run *sting operations,* where officers pose as criminal fences or drug dealers; a *john detail* is a variation used against street prostitution and cruising activities. Undercover officers differ from plainclothes officers, whose police status is known or acknowledged; an undercover officer's police identity is secret.

Internal Affairs. Internal Affairs, sometimes called the Office of Professional Responsibility or a similar title, is the most specialized investigative function. It has the responsibility for investigating allegations of crime and misconduct by other police officers in the organization. *Juvenile investigations* is both an investigative unit specializing in juvenile crime and a support unit that works with social service agencies to get juvenile offenders back on the straight and narrow.

Other specialties exist. Only a few cities have full-time SWAT (Special Weapons and Tactics) squads, but many have trained personnel who can be mobilized into a team if needed; smaller cities and towns often participate in regional SWAT teams. Hostage negotiations and barricaded persons situations are typical situations for SWAT. HAZMAT is a similar specialty, requiring additional training and equipment. Agencies near large bodies of water often have marine units for monitoring water traffic and for rescue. Training is a vital element of any agency for preparing new recruits, updating veterans on changes in law and procedure, and introducing new techniques and technologies to all members of the agency. In some departments, crime scene technicians are sworn officers; in others, they are civilian. School resource officers are similar to juvenile officers, but work exclusively in the schools, providing a combination of security, investigation, and public relations. They may deal exclusively with students or may have responsibilities for both student and staff conduct. D.A.R.E. is a special form of school liaison, a national antidrug curriculum taught by uniformed police officers.

Historical Background

Historically and legally, police power is vested in the community and wielded through whatever form of local government has existed:

village council, tribal chief, or feudal lord. Individuals have obligations to the community that are commonly understood. Formal policing forms are created and changed as a result of larger social changes. Full-time, paid police agencies are a relatively new development; the first modern police started in England in 1829. American policing developed out of English models.

The oldest forms of policing, the constable and the sheriff, date at least to the ninth century. When crime was relatively infrequent, the general populace could be roused by the *hue and cry* ("Stop, thief!") and obliged to pursue the felon to justice. In 1285, amid great social instability and turmoil at the close of the Crusades, England's Statute of Winchester required that all able-bodied men maintain weapons and serve in the *Watch* to protect villages and towns from fire and from outlaws. A yearlong turn as the unpaid constable, responsible for bringing lawbreakers before the King's Courts, also became compulsory.

During the 1700s, England underwent a period of rapid transformations in agriculture, technology, manufacturing, and commerce known as the Industrial Revolution. People migrated to the cities in search of jobs and urban populations expanded dramatically. Crime and disorder became rampant and mob violence was a constant threat. Small, localized *private police* forces were paid to guard parishes (neighborhoods), toll roads, docks, and warehouses, replacing the unpaid and largely ineffective Watch. Their modern-day descendants are the professional security forces and the special police forces.

Social unrest intensified after the Napoleonic Wars in the early 1800s and the English elite sought ways to suppress or defuse the unemployed, desperate "dangerous classes" that haunted the English cities. The military was the only available force capable of dealing with a riot until a reform movement brought Sir Robert Peel to power as prime minister.

In 1829, Peel established the first modern police force, the *Metropolitan London Police*. Organized along military lines and in military-like uniforms to allay fears of a "secret police" (a legacy of the secret network of informers during the French Revolution), the Bobbies were unarmed. They were primarily intelligence gatherers, getting to know the residents and conditions of a specific area and reporting back to a central administration through a chain of command. When news of trouble was discovered, large numbers of police would flood the area to forestall the violence. Over the years, their peacekeeping duties were established on a reputation for fairness and firmness.

The American Experience

English colonists brought to America the common law and the institutions of constables, county sheriffs, and the Watch. Official duties centered on the maintenance of roads and bridges, fire prevention and detection, and the service of writs for civil court matters; "crime fighting" was a minor duty. On the American frontiers of the colonial and Wild West periods, where formal institutions of government were weak, Committees of Vigilance defended isolated communities from raiders, horse thieves, and other predators. Though *vigilantes* also had a dark side in some locations, the vigilance committees were generally socially constructive, reflecting the older community self-defense modes.

American urbanization lagged behind England, but by the 1840s, conditions in U.S. cities were much like those in England. The idea of a police force was adopted, but it took a radically different form. For instance, Boston had a small "police force" under the city marshal in 1832, but its duties were more like those of today's boards of health than modern police departments.

Scholars speak of three eras of American policing: the Political Era of the nineteenth century, the Professional Era of the first half of the twentieth century, and the Community Policing Era of the late twentieth and early twenty-first centuries.

Political Era

American ward ("machine") politics reflected contests for power between ethnic groups and was built on the *patronage* system (awarding city jobs in return for political support). Political ward bosses had far more clout than supervisors in the chain of command. The police of the era were often unskilled and corrupt. With no job security unless their patron remained in office, they were more loyal to the person who provided their livelihood than to any abstract notion of "rule of law."

The police were also the instrument of entrenched capitalist interests in the early days of the Labor Movement. Police were used as strikebreakers, and clashes with striking laborers were often violent. The Pennsylvania State Constabulary, the first modern state police agency, was created in 1905 to deal with striking miners.

Professional Era

The good-government Progressive Movement of the late nineteenth century sought to reform patronage politics. The Pendleton Act of 1883 established the federal *civil service,* under which public jobs were held on the basis of merit regardless of political view. States quickly created their own civil service laws, though machine politics and patronage survived in some cities into the latter half of the twentieth century. When the Progressive Movement ceased to be part of the American political scene, a vanguard of police leaders continued to promote *professionalism* within the police service.

Police leaders advocated professionalism based upon education, training, and scientific crime detection methods. August Vollmer, the Chief of Police in Berkeley, California, instituted many innovations, including the first crime lab. His protégé, O. W. Wilson, was police chief in several cities and, as Commissioner of the Chicago Police Department, he established the fundamental principles of police administration in the early 1960s.

Professionalism was stunted by the Boston Police Strike of 1919. When one of the nation's most professional departments went on strike for higher wages (Boston officers were paid less than streetcar drivers), riots broke out. The Union Movement, with its socialist origins, was linked to the "Red Scare" of the Bolshevik Revolution that was being fought in Russia at that time. Governor Calvin Coolidge declared that "there is no right to strike against the public safety by anybody, anytime, anywhere" and called out the Massachusetts state militia to police the city. The striking officers were fired, and the movement for police unionism collapsed until the 1960s. Police remained low-paid, largely uneducated, and ill-trained. As a result, bootleggers' money in the Prohibition era was used to corrupt the local police in many areas, allowing illegal import and sale of alcohol. Promotions and assignments often were based upon seniority and favoritism, rather than merit. The 1931 Wickersham Commission reported on the brutality of police methods. *Police brutality* would resurface as one of the central themes of the most recent period of social unrest, the 1960s.

The development of federal law enforcement in the twentieth century was most visible in the development of the Federal Bureau of Investigation under its most famous director, J. Edgar Hoover. A canny use of publicity helped forge the "law enforcement" image of the police, especially against the gangland murderers of the Prohibition era (such as Al Capone) and the bank robbers of the Depression (Bonnie and Clyde, Pretty Boy Floyd, John Dillinger, Ma Barker's gang, and others).

Critics blame three things for the failure of the professional model of policing. One of these is the isolation of the squad car, which discouraged police interaction with the public. Another is the overreach and overdependence upon 9-1-1 systems, which relinquished control of the police mission to those who were not as competent to direct it. Finally, there was increased emphasis on felony-level crime because it was seen as the only "real" police work, with reliance on the UCR crime rate as the only true measure of police effectiveness. After the problems of the 1960s, dissatisfactions with the professional model led to calls for community policing, under which police would focus on improving citizen satisfaction with police services, reducing fear of crime, improving quality-of-life problems, and enhancing community-building efforts.

Community Policing Era

Four major social trends converged during the 1960s and early 1970s, and the police played important roles in many of them. Social individualism was asserted in many ways, such as in challenges to mandatory school prayer, the Free Speech Movement, the rock and roll and folk-song protest and "free love" mentality of the hippie, and the emergence of the women's and gay rights movements. This individualism challenged reigning social mores. Most police were socially and politically conservative, viewing these developments with distaste and alarm and often using extralegal tactics to suppress them.

At the same time that police were being criticized for a rising crime rate, a series of landmark cases ruled upon during the 1960s reasserted the rights of accused individuals and curtailed the powers of the police. The *Mapp v. Ohio* Fourth Amendment search-and-seizure case extended the *exclusionary rule* to state courts in 1961. *Miranda v. Arizona* in 1966 required the police to inform criminal suspects in custodial interrogation of their Fifth Amendment rights against self-incrimination.

The civil rights movement for racial equality marked the beginning of the 1960s and more violent protests and rhetoric, and the urban riots of 1965 to 1968 dominated the public consciousness. News footage documented police violence against peaceful protestors to break up demonstrations. Police inaction and occasional collusion in crimes committed against blacks and civil rights workers were publicly known or suspected. Police actions precipitated many of the urban riots in the mid-1960s: in August 1965 in the Watts district of Los Angeles; in July 1965 in Newark, New Jersey; in July 1965 in Detroit. Federal law enforcement was often in opposition to local police during this era. For example, U.S. marshals protected African American children who were integrating local schools, and the FBI investigated crimes against the black community.

The antiwar movement protesting U.S. military involvement in Vietnam began with draft-eligible college students, who were initially marginalized as cowards, traitors, and communist sympathizers. After the Tet offensive in January 1968, however, opposition to the war grew rapidly. The actions of the Chicago police against demonstrators at the August 1968 Democratic National Convention were heavily covered by the media, which showcased police brutality to a nationwide television audience.

Police ineffectiveness at curbing crime, insensitivity to civil rights, and isolation from the community produced a crisis of public confidence in the police. Presidential commissions examined the causes of the urban riots and the widespread criticism of the police. The 1967 report of the President's Commission on Law Enforcement and the Administration of Justice found the police were poorly educated, poorly trained, poorly equipped, and poorly led. The federal government embarked on an improvement program under the 1968 Omnibus Crime Control and Safe Streets Act. Through the Law Enforcement Assistance Administration (LEAA), the government spent millions of dollars to improve police equipment and training. The Law Enforcement Education Program (LEEP) financed college education for both serving officers and prospective officers.

During the 1970s, some police agencies began researching their operations in the hope that scientific validation would improve their resources, but the early results were a shock. The *Kansas City Preventive Patrol Experiment* suggested that routine police patrol had almost no effect on crime, fear of crime, citizen awareness of the police, or citizen confidence. Rapid response was found to have little impact on crime except for the rare instances when a crime was reported in progress. Contrary to the image projected in television shows and movies, a multi-city study of detective work revealed that most crimes were solved by, or on the basis of, work done by uniformed patrol officers. Detectives mostly did the paperwork for court.

New approaches to policing emerged in the late 1970s and early 1980s. Herman Goldstein criticized the police for being concerned with the means of policing over the ends that policing might accomplish. He proposed that the police focus instead on problem-oriented approaches. Building upon the experiences of the *Flint (Michigan) Neighborhood Foot Patrol Program,* others began asserting the need for community-oriented policing that emphasized greater contact between police and citizens than was possible in motorized patrol.

At the current time, the community policing model contends with two alternate viewpoints: a resurgent professional model that includes "zero tolerance" policing and a CompStat model of administration (to be discussed). Ironically, each of the models looks to the so-called Broken Windows theory for legitimacy and to problem-solving approaches for tactics.

"Broken Windows: The Police and Neighborhood Safety" is the title of an article by Wilson and Kelling that was published in 1982. Its central metaphor was the broken window that goes unrepaired, signaling that "no one cares" about an abandoned property and inviting further vandalism. Extending the metaphor to public disorder, such as drug sales, drunkenness, and prostitution, the authors argued that the police should be more attentive to conditions signaling that an area is ripe for criminal plunder. The article advocated "order-maintenance policing," a focus on the "small things" that the police had traditionally overlooked because they were not serious felony crimes. "Broken Windows" became the foundation for two distinct, but complementary, changes in police practice: problem-oriented and community-oriented policing.

Problem-Oriented Policing. Problem-oriented policing (POP) emphasizes analysis of crimes and situations, looking for patterns that may cross categorical lines. It seeks specific causes that may give rise to multiple events and fashions solutions to the causes, not the symptoms. Unlike order-maintenance policing, POP extends beyond the police service, integrating appropriate roles from other criminal justice, social service, and private agencies, as indicated by the problem analysis.

Community-Oriented Policing. Community-oriented policing (COP) distinguishes itself from the traditional professional model in several ways. First, it recognizes that the police have responsibilities for a wide variety of noncrime conditions, some of which may be criminogenic (crime-producing) and some merely annoying. Abandoned buildings, trash-strewn lots, and barking dogs are not considered "real" police work, but they remain matters of great concern to neighbors because they diminish the quality of life for community residents. The "Broken Windows" rationale linked quality-of-life issues to the potential for criminal incidents, making them legitimate police concerns. The police have been a powerful catalyst, organizing communities to act on their own behalf and effectively mobilizing other resources, such as health and housing inspectors, public works, nonprofit agencies, and many other strategies to help abate problem conditions in communities.

Second, community policing includes community representatives in the decision-making processes of the police department. Formal advisory boards at the agency and precinct level help to establish priorities for action. Police participation in neighborhood meetings provides two-way communication of information and concerns.

The 1982 Flint Neighborhood Foot Patrol Program demonstrated a marked improvement in citizen satisfaction with police who patrolled their neighborhoods on foot, even though the actual crime rate had changed little. Similar results were found in foot patrol and fear-reduction projects in Houston, Texas, and Newark, New Jersey, in the same time period. With the success of early problem-solving efforts in Newport News, Virginia, those efforts coalesced into a community policing movement that looked for more than simple law enforcement.

The ultimate goal of community policing is a safer community. That goal is also sought by professional-model policing, but community policing proponents seek to build and maintain a community capacity to self-regulate the conduct of residents and visitors without resorting to the enforcement arm of the police except in extreme, and ideally rare, cases.

As a philosophical umbrella, COP stresses routine nonemergency interaction between police officers and the communities they serve. By breaking down previous barriers of mistrust, this approach provides a sound foundation for mutual problem-solving efforts, helps develop critical information about individuals and conditions in the neighborhoods, and ultimately leads to greater citizen participation in law compliance and crime prevention. In practice, community policing initiatives have ranged from half-hearted failures to innovative and highly effective programs. COP has been a new label for old programs such as crime prevention, community relations, and even enhanced patrol. It has also been a vehicle for an entirely new approach to policing, which includes the community as an active partner in public safety. The wide range and mixed effectiveness of local COP initiatives leads critics to question whether the claims of community policing are merely rhetoric, or a new reality.

Resurgent Professionalism emerged as the police culture resisted some of the changes demanded by community policing. Many officers, supervisors, and agencies still consider law enforcement to be their primary mission-deterring criminals through aggressive patrol and arresting those who are not deterred. Some reject community policing precepts outright as "not police work"; others may recognize the inherent value of the activities, but conclude that they are too labor-intensive and time-consuming in the face of overwhelming demands for police service and shrinking resources.

Professionally oriented police take their inspiration from New York City's dramatic crime decrease in the mid-1990s under Commissioner William Bratton. The NYPD mounted an aggressive campaign against low-level law violations that had previously been ignored: sidewalk drug sales, loitering, turnstile-jumping in the subways, loud music, public drinking, and so on. Police culture christened this approach "zero tolerance" after an earlier U.S. Customs drug interdiction program, under the catchphrase "If you take care of the little things [disorder], the big things [crime] will take care of themselves."

At a practical level, the zero tolerance version of order-maintenance policing translates into "arrest as many people as possible for as many things as possible." It is not always done that way, of course, but it allows the police to focus on the arrest-law enforcement-as the primary crime-fighting tool, to the exclusion of the "softer" community-building duties of community policing. As originally conceived, however, order maintenance policing has a much broader mandate than just "arrest 'em all and let the courts sort it out." The original "Broken Windows" prescription looked at arrest as a last resort. Setting and enforcing local rules of civility and conduct were more important to true order-maintenance policing. A zero tolerance campaign may help restore order in hard-pressed areas, but it is not necessarily a long-term strategy that will restore community competence.

CompStat was the other major factor of the NYPD experience. Briefly put, CompStat was the use of weekly statistics as a basis for police operations, rather than simply responding to 9-1-1 calls. Police administrators were held to account for the conditions in their precincts, and that accountability in turn drove the targeted police actions on the street.

Not everyone believes that aggressive law enforcement was solely responsible for the drop in crime in New York. More cautious scholars note that many other cities experienced a downturn in crime during the same period without anything like the dramatic focus of CompStat or aggressive street policing. Others note that CompStat fueled a police crackdown, directing increased resources at problems that previously had been ignored. Such crackdowns usually produce dramatic reductions in crime or other activity, but the reductions are seldom long-term. There are additional concerns that aggressive police actions serve to alienate the community rather than enlist it as a partner, and that an enforcement-based faith in deterrence forfeits the benefits of other crime-prevention approaches.

Enduring Elements and Issues

Across the multiple types and approaches to policing are certain themes common to the American police. Many of them center on what scholars call the *police subculture,* the views of the world shared by many police officers. Police discretion, the use of force, corruption, their handling of special constituencies, and the relations with the community, particularly minority citizens, are all intertwined in this hard-to-define concept.

Police Subculture

The idea of a police subculture that was at odds with mainstream society stems from the politically charged era of the 1960s. Two schools of thought emerged to explain the adversarial relationships of the day. Police opponents viewed the overwhelmingly Caucasian, almost entirely male police as racist, ignorant, authoritarian, and thuggish, completely out of touch with a changing society. In this viewpoint, police work attracted mean-spirited bullies.

The other school of thought held that people were drawn to police work out of a sense of altruism, but the nature of police work transformed them. The major scholars of the police of the 1960s drew a picture of police whose "working personality" was marked by concepts of danger, authority, and cynicism. The nature of officers' work meant dealing with people at their worst, handling problems of abuse and death on a regular basis, being personally reviled, and having their motives questioned. These situations combined to harden police officers, who began to respond differently as a defense mechanism. Those scholars also noted that the police were prone to use stereotypes as a "perceptual shorthand" to discern and minimize danger by "seeing" a profile, not a person.

The wider admission of women and minorities to policing has had some effect on police culture, but certain common themes are still recognized. Police officers work within a moral framework as much as a legal one, assessing situations on the basis of the persons involved. A feeling of "us against them" predominates in many areas, though community policing often bridges that barrier. Crank (1998) summarized many of the themes of police culture. One theme is the necessity and righteousness of force. Another is reliance upon an undefined "common sense" and personal bravery in the face of sudden and potential danger. A third is a moral division of the world into "good" and "bad" people, with the police as a "thin blue line" between civilization and chaos. Other themes include solidarity in the face of opposition, individualism and personal autonomy, unpredictability, and survival.

Because most officers are socially and politically conservative, the police culture adapts slowly and sometimes grudgingly to changes in the social and legal environment. Guyot (1979) likened the process of creating change in police organizations to "bending granite." This resistance often puts the police at odds with large segments of the public, as it did in the 1960s, and gives rise to a series of concerns about police behavior. Common to all of the concerns is the manner in which police exercise their discretion.

Police Corruption

Corruption is the use of the police position for personal gain. Although it is common to refer to police powers as those of arrest and the right to use force, police discretion also gives the police the power *not* to arrest, and indeed not to take action at all. In the nineteenth and early twentieth centuries, with police salaries as low as the hiring standards, police were susceptible to bribes to "look the other way," "lose" evidence, or focus their enforcement efforts on a business competitor. During Prohibition, bootleggers bribed police in cities on a widespread basis. In modern times, higher standards and better salaries have improved the police as a whole, but pockets of corruption are revealed periodically.

More problematic than the bribing of police by organized crime are the cases in which the police themselves become criminals. The classic case in modern times was "The Pad" in New York City, revealed by Frank Serpico to the Knapp Commission in the early 1970s. Systematic police corruption shook down merchants for protection money like the racketeers of earlier periods. Shaking down drug dealers, confiscating their drugs, and selling the drugs themselves have been a problem in several cities, as uncovered by the Mollen Commission's investigation of NYPD corruption in the 1980s and the Los Angeles Ramparts Division CRASH scandal of the late 1990s.

Harassment

The idea of a clear-cut moral division of the world focuses police attention on those they deem "bad." Those whose appearance or behavior signals "trouble" are likely to be subjected to scrutiny, usually in a field interrogation contact to determine who they are and what they are up to. Constant police pressure on violent street gangs and drug dealers is considered a good thing, serving the law-abiding citizens by reducing the opportunity for the criminals to act out. When the net is widened to include law-abiding citizens whose demeanor is without reproach and who bear only a superficial resemblance to the criminals, however, the police affront the autonomy and personal dignity of citizens. If that happens on a regular basis, the perception grows that the police are merely harassing people they do not like.

Racial profiling is a recent development, arising from police efforts to intercept bulk drugs before they can be marketed in the cities. Cases in New Jersey and Maryland documented that state police stopped and searched minority motorists' cars in numbers far greater than their proportion of highway users. The underlying assumption equating race with criminality-the belief that African Americans and Hispanics are more involved with drug trafficking than whites-was not borne out by the search results. Drugs were found at equal rates in minority and white motorists' cars. Other jurisdictions have found similar patterns of racial disparities in stops, though in less dramatic numbers. The fundamental objection is to the use of race rather than behavior as a reason for initiating a police inquiry. Other objections arise from the manner in which minority motorists are treated during the contact.

Improper Use of Force and Police Brutality

The power to use "non-negotiably coercive force" in defense of the law and social order is vital to the police role. Across the vast landscape of police-citizen interactions, police use force properly, if at all-most incidents are resolved without force. Like any other power, however, it can be subject to abuse. There are two primary categories of abuse. *Wrongful use* involves applying force for the wrong reason, such as to retaliate against a person for "disrespect" to the officer. *Disproportionate use* occurs when the level of force far exceeds the level of resistance or aggression of the subject. The police are also required to protect the life and safety of those they use force against, once the situation is brought under control.

Legitimate force may be used to bring resisting subjects into compliance. This usually requires them to submit to arrest, although people may also be forced out of areas where they are trespassing. Police are trained and equipped to employ force in accordance with the *force continuum,* which links the level of police force to the aggressiveness and resistance of the citizen. Federal funding has promoted the development of less lethal weaponry to assist the police in their mission yet minimize the risk of harm to officers, suspects, and bystanders. Incapacitating chemical agents, such as pepper spray, beanbag rounds that knock a person down but do not penetrate the skin, capture nets fired from a shotgun, sticky-foam, disorienting lights and stun grenades, and other weapons still in the development stage all seek to provide a safer alternative to gunfire.

Police have the power to use deadly force only to save their own lives or those of a third party. A common-law "fleeing felon" rule allowed lethal force to apprehend any accused felon. In 1985, the U.S. Supreme Court in *Tennessee v. Garner* restricted the use of lethal force to situations of imminent and articulable danger. Although police sidearms are the most obvious instruments of lethal force, blunt objects such as the baton or nightstick are also capable of inflicting deadly harm, such as a blow to the head, if used improperly, or against the wrong target.

Periodically, the issue of improper use of force is brought to the public's attention by a high-profile case. The celebrated case of the beating of Rodney King by Los Angeles police officers was partially captured on videotape. Part of the incident involved legitimate use of force to take a resisting suspect into custody. At some point, many feel the event turned into an episode of street justice, the extralegal use of physical force as a punishment for "contempt of cop." The police community is split over whether only some of the force was illegitimate, or all was legitimate, and over whether there were alternative tactics that could have been used.

The Abner Louima case in New York City shocked the nation, as an out-of-control police officer sexually assaulted a prisoner with a stick because he thought the man had punched him in a street scuffle. This was a clear-cut case of brutality, personal abuse of authority to avenge a perceived personal affront. The Amadou Diallo case is more problematic. Diallo was confronted in the early morning by four armed plainclothes officers searching for a rape suspect. An immigrant with poor English skills, he reached for his wallet, which appeared to the officers as an attempt to draw a weapon. The officers fired a total of 41 shots, killing Diallo. The issue of imminent possible danger and the need to make a split-second decision in defense of themselves and their partners is a major factor that distinguishes the Louima and Diallo cases. The issue of racial prejudice is an element in both cases, as in the Rodney King incident and many fatal shootings, because the situation involved black suspects and white officers.

The Blue Wall

The cultural theme of feeling unappreciated and under fire combines with themes of danger and solidarity to create the *Blue Wall of Silence*. Police officers who know of wrongdoing by other police will not take action against them or provide information against them to investigators because of two things. First, police mistrust their superiors and fear being given disproportionately harsh punishment to set an example or to alleviate political pressure on their administrators.

Second, they fear alienating their brother and sister officers, upon whom they depend for backup assistance in dangerous situations. Unions also fear that employee rights will be abrogated under political pressure, so they will intervene as advocates and lawyers for officers accused of wrongdoing. To the public, it appears that "the police protect their own," even against legitimate grievances and complaints of the community. The Blue Wall is no longer as strong as it was once thought to be. Professional and community-oriented officers realize that the police must clean their own house for legitimacy and that a rogue officer is as much a danger to them as the criminals.

Policing the Police

The periodic scandals that arise from police misconduct are followed by public cries for police reform. In the past, most reforms were promises of better internal management by the police agency. In effect, clear rules would be written, better training would be devised, and supervision would be stricter. Police agencies asserted that the illegal behavior featured in the headlines was solely confined to the "bad apples" and not representative of the majority of police officers, who were honest, fair, and devoted to the public good.

More recently, the cyclical nature of police scandals has led people to question the ability of the police to police themselves. Because criminal convictions of police officers are difficult to obtain, aggrieved citizens and advocacy groups have pursued lawsuits against police agencies for denial of civil rights. In addition, the federal Justice Department has moved against some police departments, using lawsuits to craft *consent decrees* that articulate specific changes the departments must make. Typically, those changes are monitored by an outside entity that reports to the federal court; the issue of racial profiling by the New Jersey State Police resulted in one such consent decree.

Federal intervention depends upon the willingness of the current administration to intervene. Lawsuits can also take years to settle. At the local level, residents concerned with police misconduct have begun to call for *civilian review* of police. Allegations of police misconduct are heard by boards composed entirely of residents or a mixture of residents and police officials. Conduct is judged based upon community expectations rather than just police practice. In the best models, police experts identify the acceptable standards and types of training that support police policy. The judgments made are then based on whether or not the officers' conduct was in accordance with law, with policy, and with community expectations of conduct. If discipline is recommended, typically the police chief is responsible for its administration.

Special Constituencies

Police often face issues regarding communities with special needs. Mentally ill individuals are much more prominent on the streets of the nation in the wake of the deinstitutionalization movement in the 1950s that closed asylums and hospitals. Their behavior may be frightening to citizens, and some are potentially dangerous. Immigrant communities bring new languages, different social customs and expectations, and often an antagonism toward the police, which is based upon their experiences with extremely corrupt and brutal police in their homelands. Police often lack the language skills and social understanding to make contact with these communities, thus hindering service. In both cases, individuals are also vulnerable targets for criminals who take advantage of the person's inability or reluctance to communicate with the police. In addition, community policing attempts to establish positive relations with immigrants are often in conflict with the federal laws and enforcement mandates to deport those illegally in the country. Some local agencies do not cooperate with the Immigration and Naturalization Service (INS) because cooperation would inhibit their ability to protect the legitimate immigrant community. Other agencies complain that when they do apprehend illegal immigrants, the understaffed INS cannot take them into custody and the police are forced to release them. The elderly are also emerging as a new concern for police, who have to deal with issues such as Alzheimer's disease, dementia, isolation, and loneliness.

Future Issues

At the time of this writing, the aftermath of the attacks on the World Trade Center and the Pentagon on September 11, 2001, holds the potential for dramatic changes in the nation's police. The creation of the *Homeland Security Department* at the cabinet level combined many smaller federal enforcement functions under a single office.

Racial profiling, particularly of Arabs, has received new social support despite the continuing problems of African American and Hispanic profiling domestically. Immigration rules are being tightened and enforcement increased, but the same problems remain for police who must deal with local immigrant communities. Civil liberties are threatened in exchange for what is believed to be greater security against terror.

Technology also poses many new challenges for the police. Computer fraud and identity theft are new forms of theft for which most police agencies are not prepared. They lack the necessary state-of-the-art equipment and only a handful of officers have the necessary skills to track cyberspace looters, hackers, and other electronic predators. The very notion of jurisdiction changes in cyberspace, and American laws often conflict with laws of the European Union, China, and others.

Invasive technologies may soon be widely available, threatening traditional expectations of privacy. The case of *Kyllo v. United States* required the police to observe privacy as it existed in 1789 when the Constitution was adopted, banning the police use of any new technologies that revealed intimate details of a house (such as thermal imagers, which were used in the Kyllo case). That technology may soon be widely available to the public and to the criminal element, however, requiring both new investigative skills and new counter-measures to protect police resources. Implanted chips, cloning, live human-computer interface, augmented reality systems, and many more technologies are raising long-term and potentially profound issues that the police will have to face.

Social expectations are also changing. The nation's punitive drug laws are again coming under attack as too harsh, wrongly applied, and the wrong approach to the problems of drug abuse. The nature of privacy in public spaces is being redefined by closed-circuit TV and other technologies. The line dividing federal and state rights is being redefined in the states' favor by the Supreme Court at the same time that many state crimes are being "federalized" in hopes of securing harsher penalties. The impact of globalization upon the economy, laws, and social expectations of the nation-indeed, in a longer view, even upon the concept of the nation-state and sovereignty-has not fully been realized. Globalization is a long-term force with short-term ripples. The "War on Terror" may be a short-term problem, but it has long-term implications for civil rights and civil liberties. Technology has implications for both and presents an even more uncertain future as the definition of what it is to be human is determined. All of these present the possibility of another period of radical change for the police, adjusting to new factors in the human and social condition.

References

Bittner, E. (1970). *The functions of the police in modern society: A review of background factors, current practices, and possible role models.* Cambridge, MA: MIT Press.

Crank, J. P. (1998). *Understanding police culture.* Cincinnati, OH: Anderson.

Guyot, D. (1979). Bending granite: Attempts to change the rank structure of American police departments. *Journal of Police Science and Administration, 7* (3), 253–284.

Kyllo v. United States, U.S. Supreme Court No. 99-8508 (June 2001).

Mapp v. Ohio, 367 U.S. 643 (1961).

Miranda v. Arizona, 384 U.S. 436, 446 (1966).

President's Commission on Law Enforcement and the Administration of Justice. (1967). *The challenge of crime in a free society.* Washington, DC: Government Printing Office.

Tennessee V. Garner, 471 U.S. 105 S. Ct. 1694 (1985).

Wilson, J. Q. (1968). *Varieties of police behavior: The management of law and order in eight communities.* Cambridge, MA: Harvard University Press.

Wilson, J. Q., & Kelling, G. L. (1982, March). Broken windows: The police and neighborhood safety. *The Atlantic Monthly,* pp. 29–38.

Suggested Readings

Police Culture

Crank, J. P., & Caldero, M. A. (2000). *Police ethics: The corruption of noble cause.* Cincinnati, OH: Anderson.

Muir, W. K., Jr. (1977). *Police: Streetcorner politicians.* Chicago: University of Chicago Press.

Community-Oriented and Problem-Oriented Policing

Goldstein, H. (1979). Improving policing: A problem-oriented approach. *Crime and Delinquency, 25,* 236–258.

Greene, J. R., & Mastrofski, S. D. (Eds.). (1988). *Community policing: Rhetoric or reality.* New York: Praeger.

Sparrow, M., Moore, M. H., & Kennedy, D. (1990). *Beyond 9-1-1: A new era for policing.* New York: Basic Books.

Trojanowicz, R., & Bucqueroux, B. (1990). *Community policing: A contemporary perspective.* Cincinnati, OH: Anderson.

Modern Reform: Initial Studies

Klockars, C. (1985). *The idea of police.* Beverly Hills, CA: Sage.

Reiss, A. J., Jr. (1971). *The police and the public.* New Haven, CT: Yale University Press.

Discussion Questions

1. This chapter described how law enforcement in the United States is the responsibility of a variety of organizations, agencies, and jurisdictions. What are some of the positive and negative consequences of having law enforcement decentralized in this manner?

2. Federal law enforcement underwent rapid changes after the September 11, 2001, attacks at the World Trade Center and the Pentagon, with many formerly separate functions combined under the Homeland Security Department. Additionally, the U.S.A. Patriot Act and other legislation authorized increased levels of surveillance that some feel erode the traditional protections of privacy and individual rights. Drawing upon your knowledge of world and national events, discuss the possible changes in expectations of law enforcement that these developments are beginning to create. ✦

Chapter Four

Courts and Legal Issues

Key Concepts and Terms

- Adversarial System

- Assembly-Line Justice

- Burden of Proof

- Courtroom Workgroup

- Criminal Law vs. Civil Law

- Dual Court System

- Due Process vs. Crime Control

- Jurisdiction

- Presumption of Innocence

Introduction

The court system plays an integral role in the administration of criminal justice. Once a defendant has been arrested, courts are responsible for the proper adjudication of the case. If a case proceeds through all stages of the criminal justice process, the courts will be involved in most aspects of that case. Thus, it is critical to understand the role of the courts in the criminal justice system.

The role of the courts is to interpret and apply the laws of the states and the federal government. Most criminal law is enacted and enforced at the state level because, historically, states have been given the power to create their own systems of criminal law and procedure. As a result, most crimes that come to the attention of the criminal justice system are handled by state court systems. According to the Court Statistics Project (2001), state court dispositions in criminal cases numbered over 7 million in 2000 compared with the roughly 46,000 criminal cases per year decided in federal courts.

Common Law

The U.S. legal system is derived from English *common law*. In the eleventh and twelfth centuries in England, law was parochial in that judges would create law and apply the law only in local areas. In the mid- to late 1100s, application of the law was expanded to apply to entire regions. When this occurred, the law was considered common law because it was now common to everyone. Common law was judge-made law. This tradition continued through the 1600s in England, and offenses such as murder, robbery, and larceny were originally created by judges. When the colonists settled in America, they brought the common law tradition with them. Today, however, judges are not responsible for the creation of laws; elected legislatures have that responsibility.

Another feature applicable to common law is *precedent*. This means that judges make decisions on the basis of previous applications of the law in similar cases. For example, when a judge receives a case before him, he will review previous decisions that he and other judges have made to determine if a similar case has already been decided. The judge will then be guided by the previous decision when making his decision about the case. This is done to ensure that cases are decided in a consistent manner. Judges do not have to abide by precedent, however. A judge may feel that a previous decision is incorrect and will therefore rule in a different way. In general, judges abide by precedent and advocate that changes in the law should be gradual.

Sources of Law

Today, the primary source of law is the elected legislature. This includes both the fifty state legislatures (e.g., Ohio General Assembly, New York State Legislature) and the federal legislature (U.S. Congress) as well as local units of government (e.g., county commissions, city councils). Legislatures adopted the common-law crimes of murder, robbery, and others, but they also created other types of crime (e.g., white-collar crimes).

Other sources of law in the United States include the various state constitutions as well as the federal Constitution. In general, constitutions outline the structure of governments and the powers that those governments will undertake. The highest form of law in the United States is the U.S. Constitution. All laws must abide by the U.S. Constitution, according to Article VI: "This Constitution . . . shall be the Supreme Law of the Land; and the judges in every state shall be bound thereby. . . ." In effect, if any law contravenes the U.S. Constitution, that law cannot stand. States also have their own constitutions that are the highest form of law in the state; however, these constitutions must also abide by the U.S. Constitution.

Regulatory or administrative agencies are another source of law in the United States. The federal legislature creates agencies such as the Securities and Exchange Commission, which in turn creates rules and renders decisions concerning securities laws. State legislatures create agencies as well to regulate activity throughout the state. For example, the Ohio General Assembly created a Public Defender Commission to regulate the performance of the state's public defenders. According to Neubauer (2002), administrative regulations are the fastest-growing source of law in this country.

A final source of law in the United States is perhaps the oldest. As mentioned, judges were responsible for the creation of law hundreds of years ago in England. Although judges are no longer primarily responsible for the creation of law, they continue to exercise their law-making authority. When cases come before a judge, he or she is responsible for interpreting law that has been created by other sources. If a law is deemed by a judge to be faulty, the judge will direct the source of that law to change or eliminate that law. A prime example of this is seen when judges are called upon to ensure that laws comply with the U.S. Constitution. If a state legislature enacts a law that conflicts with the U.S. Constitution, it is typically the judge who directs the legislature to remedy the conflict. By directing the legislature to change its laws, judges exercise a fair amount of lawmaking authority.

Criminal Law vs. Civil Law

The law can be divided into two types: criminal and civil. Criminal and civil law are distinct from one another in that each involves a different set of rules and procedures. The *criminal law* is concerned with offenses against society as a whole, whereas *civil law* is concerned with private actions. If a criminal law is violated, it is deemed a violation of the laws of the state or the federal government, and it is the responsibility of the state or federal government to ensure that the offender is held accountable for his actions. For example, if an individual is assaulted in San Francisco, the state of California (in the form of a prosecutor) will process the offender (called a defendant) through the criminal justice system, because that assault is seen as a violation of California criminal law. In civil actions, an individual may feel she has been wronged by another and it is then her responsibility to ensure that the wrongdoer is held accountable for his actions. For example, if an individual is involved in an auto accident with another person, that individual (called a plaintiff) may sue the other person (called a defendant) in civil court in order to recoup the cost of fixing the car. In this civil case, the government is not involved because the incident does not involve a violation of criminal laws.

Although criminal and civil law are separate entities, criminal actions sometimes appear in civil court. In the assault above, the victim may sue his attacker in civil court to recover costs associated with doctors' visits or missed work. In this case, not only can the offender be punished by the State of California for violation of California law, but he can also be sued in a private action by the victim and taken to civil court.

Another distinction between criminal and civil law involves the penalties involved in criminal and civil proceedings. In criminal law, an individual is found guilty of an offense and is faced with a number of possible punishments involving deprivation of life (death sentence), deprivation of liberty (incarceration), and deprivation of property (fines). These are deemed "punishments" by the criminal law. In civil law, an individual is found liable for his actions and is faced with deprivation of property (damages). These are deemed penalties by the civil law. Civil law does not involve deprivations of life or liberty, and damages are not seen as a punishment in the sense of the criminal law.

Adversarial System

As mentioned, criminal law involves the government adjudicating cases that involve violation of a particular statute. When a defendant is processed through the system, she is faced with intense governmental scrutiny of her actions. The defendant does, however, have an opportunity to defend herself. This is what is referred to as the *adversarial* system of justice. In this system, there are two sides that present evidence and a neutral body (either a judge or jury) that decides the outcome of the case. To counter the resources that the government has on its side, a defendant is able to have an attorney assist in her defense. There is also a *presumption of innocence* on the part of the defendant, in that he is presumed innocent unless proven otherwise by the prosecutor. To do this, the prosecutor must prove the defendant is guilty "beyond a reasonable doubt," a standard that is not clearly defined. This is called the *burden of proof*. According to Steury and Frank (1996), beyond a reasonable doubt means about 95 percent certain or if there is no other reasonable interpretation of the evidence.

The defendant also has a number of protections in an adversarial system of justice. A defendant has the right to know the charges against him, the right to a speedy, public, and impartial trial, the right to obtain witnesses in his favor, and the right to cross-examine witnesses. These protections ensure that the adversarial process is preserved and that the defendant is not exposed to the inquisitorial system of justice found in many European countries. In this system, the focus is on fact-finding, and judges play a key role in finding out the truth regarding the case. To do this, a defendant gives up some protections because the focus is on discovering the truth, not necessarily ensuring the rights of the defendant.

Due Process vs. Crime Control

The focus on the rights of the defendant is inherent in the due process model of criminal justice. The *due process model* states that a defendant should not be adjudicated, convicted, or punished without basic rules of procedure being followed. This is to ensure that only the truly guilty are convicted and punished, and that innocent people do not "fall through the cracks" (see Packer, 1968).

The Fifth Amendment to the U.S. Constitution guarantees that the federal government will follow due process provisions when processing individuals through the criminal justice system, and the Fourteenth Amendment ensures that state governments follow those procedures as well. The basic due process provisions are found in the amendments to the U.S. Constitution. Table 4.1 illustrates these provisions. Packer (1968) argued that agents in the criminal justice system make mistakes, and that the due process provisions are in place to correct those mistakes to ensure fair and consistent administration of justice.

Table 4.1
Due Process Protections

4th Amendment	protection from illegal searches and seizures by the government, requirement of a warrant based on probable cause and signed by a neutral judge before a search or seizure may be undertaken
5th Amendment	federal due process and grand jury provisions, the right against self-incrimination (cannot be forced to be a witness against oneself), the right against double jeopardy (cannot be prosecuted twice for the same crime)
6th Amendment	suspect has the right to know the charges against him, the right to a speedy, impartial, and public trial, the right to confront and cross-examine witnesses who are testifying against him, the right to obtain witnesses in his own behalf, and the right to have an attorney
8th Amendment	government cannot impose excessive bail or fines, an offender is protected against cruel and unusual punishment
14th Amendment	state due process provision, all citizens are subject to the law equally (equal protection)

Conversely, it is argued that due process provisions throw a wrench into the criminal justice system by slowing down the administration of justice. The *crime control model* of criminal justice argues that individuals who come into contact with the system are more often than not guilty, and that the system should be able to provide smooth and efficient processing of cases. The crime control model favors minimal due process protections because of the belief that these may free the guilty on technicalities, thus contributing to an ineffective system of justice. The court system attempts to strike a balance between these competing models-providing an efficient, yet effective system while preserving the due process rights of defendants.

The Court System

Before looking at the structure and function of state and federal courts, it is important to outline various concepts that are featured throughout all court systems.

Dual Court System

Although we obviously have both state and federal court systems, it is important to understand that these are distinct from each other and operate under differing sets of rules and laws. Although state courts must ensure that they are following federal law and the U.S. Constitution, these courts operate under rules and procedures that are created by the state legislatures and the courts themselves. For example, the state legislature may specify that in order for an individual to serve as a judge, he must be a practicing lawyer for at least 10 years. Also, courts may create rules to which members of the court (i.e., attorneys, judges, jurors, etc.) must adhere. For example, a presiding judge may issue orders (called gag orders) to prevent trial participants from discussing a case with others.

Much of what state courts do is separate from what the federal courts do. State courts handle violations of state law; they do not handle cases involving violations of federal law. Federal courts handle violations of the federal law; they only deal with violations of state law if those laws contradict federal law or the U.S. Constitution. Most of the crimes committed in the United States are violations of state laws; thus, state courts handle the bulk of crimes committed in this country.

Jurisdiction

The term *jurisdiction* is often thought of as a particular geographic area. With regard to the court system, however, this term refers to the authority of a court to hear a case. Using general examples, state courts do not have jurisdiction to hear cases involving federal law, and criminal courts do not have jurisdiction to hear cases involving civil matters. Specifically, courts in the state of Minnesota have jurisdiction only over cases that involve violations of Minnesota law-these courts cannot hear cases that involve violations of the laws of other states. Jurisdiction allows courts to narrow the number of cases they can hear and enables courts to gain expertise about a particular subject matter.

Assembly-Line Justice

The criminal justice system has come under criticism for the way cases are moved through the system. The brunt of this criticism falls on the courts, especially lower courts. As will be discussed, lower courts handle 90 percent of all criminal cases. Lower courts are responsible for processing misdemeanor cases (the majority of all criminal cases) and handling the initial stages of felony cases (such as first appearances and preliminary hearings). In a number of states, lower courts are overloaded in that there are not enough resources to devote more than a minimal amount of time to each case. Attorneys are often juggling multiple cases at one time and are not able to focus on one case for an extended period of time. Because of this, cases are processed in the most efficient way possible to ensure that the system does not stall or become clogged. Moving the cases in this way has been referred to as assembly-line justice, because a case will move from step to step in the same way a product moves from step to step in a manufacturing assembly line.

Courtroom Workgroup

Assembly-line justice is possible partly because of the *courtroom workgroup*. The workgroup consists of the interactions among courtroom actors; in particular, judges, prosecutors, and defense attorneys. Although the criminal justice system is supposed to be adversarial, actors in the courtroom workgroup are not typical adversaries. In courts with heavy caseloads, the courtroom workgroup comes together to dispose of cases in an efficient manner. The actors in a workgroup have shared goals and will work together to achieve those goals. For example, a prosecutor wants quick convictions, a defense attorney wants fair but quick resolution of his case, and a judge wants prompt agreement on a disposition. The workgroup is most successful when the actors have worked together for a period of time and are aware of the practices and abilities of each other. The workgroup is sometimes upset by additions to a courtroom; for instance, a defense attorney may move to another courtroom or a judge may no longer hear certain types of cases. Because of this, the remaining actors in the workgroup must get to know the new actors to determine if they share similar goals. If not, cases may not be disposed of in a manner that emphasizes assembly-line justice.

Attrition and Plea Bargaining

Coupled with efficient disposition of cases are the concepts of case attrition and plea bargaining. These are needed to ensure that the assembly line continues in overloaded courts. *Attrition* refers to the elimination of cases in the system, usually in the early stages of a case. Attrition occurs for many reasons, such as dismissal of the charges (due to lack of evidence or witness problems), formal policies such as priority prosecution that focus resources on certain types of cases, and personal standards of justice. In the last scenario, prosecutors may not bring charges against a defendant if the prosecutor does not feel the offense is serious enough to warrant charges. Thus, attrition is mostly the result of discretionary practices by the actors in the court system, primarily prosecutors.

The guilty plea is a widely used method of case disposition, occurring in 85 to 90 percent of cases (Steury & Frank, 1996). *Plea bargaining* involves a defendant pleading guilty to an offense in exchange for lenient treatment, which could include a reduction of the charges or a reduction of the sentence. A defendant can also enter a plea of no contest (also called nolo contendere) to a charge. This means that a defendant agrees to accept the punishment for a particular behavior without having to admit guilt. A guilty plea is seen by many as a necessary evil in a system that has become increasingly overcrowded. By encouraging and accepting guilty pleas, the court system ensures not only convictions, but also that cases are disposed of quickly and that the system moves forward in an efficient manner. Critics, however, contend that reduced punishments are not appropriate for the crimes that are committed and that some defendants "get off easy."

Federal Court System

As mentioned earlier, the federal court system handles violations of federal law. Historically, federal courts owe their creation to the U.S. Constitution and Congress. The U.S. Constitution, in Article III, only specifies the creation of the U.S. Supreme Court and allows Congress to create the lower federal courts when needed: "The judicial power of the United States, shall be vested in one supreme court, and in such inferior courts as the Congress may, from time to time, ordain and establish." After the U.S. Constitution was ratified, the first bill that Congress addressed dealt with the establishment of the lower federal courts. In the Judiciary Act of 1789, Congress created three circuit courts, which functioned as appellate courts, and 13 district courts, which functioned as trial courts. The circuit courts represented three geographical districts—southern, middle, and eastern—which consisted of one district court judge and two U.S. Supreme Court Justices, who would travel to the district to hear cases twice a year (called circuit riding). The district courts were state-contained, with one district court located in each state.

Today, the federal court system does not resemble the system as it was originally created, and this is mainly the result of the reform of the circuit courts, which will subsequently be discussed. Currently, there are three major types of courts in the federal system.

First, the *U.S. district courts* are called the trial courts of the federal court system. There are currently 94 U.S. district courts in the federal system—90 within the United States and 4 in the territories of Guam, Puerto Rico, the Virgin Islands, and the Northern Mariana Islands. There is at least one U.S. district court in every state, but larger states such as California, New York, and Texas have more than one. U.S. district courts are felony trial courts, but these courts handle more civil cases than criminal cases. For example, prisoner litigation is an area of civil law that U.S. district courts are increasingly handling. U.S. district courts have *original jurisdiction,* which means that a court has the authority to hear a case and decide it.

The early circuit courts were transformed into the *U.S. Courts of Appeal* in 1891. The burden of circuit riding and a massive increase in caseload after the Civil War led Congress to reform the circuit courts into a more workable solution. With the creation of the U.S. Courts of Appeal, circuit riding was eliminated, and a more organized system for hearing cases was formed. Today, the country is divided into 11 circuits (a term left over from the earlier courts), and each circuit consists of multiple states. There is one U.S. Court of Appeal in each circuit, which is identified as the United States Court of Appeal for the Fifth Circuit or the Fifth Circuit Court of Appeal, for example. There are two other federal appellate courts: one represents the D.C. Circuit (Washington, D.C.) and one represents the Federal Circuit, which handles cases involving international trade and federal administrative law. The U.S. Courts of Appeal handle appeals from the lower district courts. As a result, they have *appellate jurisdiction,* which means they have the power to review decisions by lower courts. Most federal appeals end at the U.S. Courts of Appeal, because only a small percentage of appeals are heard by the U.S. Supreme Court.

In the federal system, the *U.S. Supreme Court* has been called the court of last resort. Cases that come before the U.S. Supreme Court involve questions of federal law (including the U.S. Constitution), and when the Court makes a decision, a party must abide by that ruling. The U.S. Supreme Court has both original and appellate jurisdiction, so it is not a typical appellate court. The Court has original jurisdiction in cases involving disputes between two states or between the federal government and a state. The overwhelming majority of the Court's cases come from lower courts, making it primarily a court with appellate jurisdiction. The U.S. Supreme Court exercises a large amount of discretion regarding the cases it chooses to hear, as it cannot possibly hear every case that comes before it. According to Neubauer (2002), the Court typically selects cases that involve important policy questions, such as those in which laws are in conflict with one another.

The role of the federal courts in the criminal justice system is limited when compared with the role of state courts. The federal courts handle special cases, such as those involving high-level drug offenders and white-collar crime, but the bulk of criminal cases is handled by the state courts. Despite this, the federal court caseload has dramatically increased in the past decade, fueled by civil rights cases, prisoner petitions, and drug offenses.

State Court Systems

When the federal court system was created by the U.S. Constitution and the Judiciary Act of 1789, state court systems were already in place. Early colonial and state courts were simplified versions of the English courts. As populations grew, court systems became more complex, especially after the Civil War. Industrialization and the growth of urban areas led to an increase in the amount of cases that state courts handled, and the courts had a difficult time adjusting to the new types of cases they were asked to hear. Because of this, new courts sprung up whenever and wherever they were needed, and this led to organizational problems. Each court was independent of the others, and there was no centralizing authority that organized and administered a unified court system. This led to changes in many states, but other states are still struggling with unification issues. As a result, the following discussion focuses on the general organization of most state court systems.

The lower courts in a state system are called *trial courts of limited jurisdiction*. These courts make up 85 percent of all judicial bodies in the United States and handle 75 percent of cases filed in state courts (Neubauer, 2002). In different states, these courts are called district, city, magistrate, or municipal courts, and all have original jurisdiction. These courts handle the early stages of felony cases (first appearance, preliminary hearings) as well as conduct trials in misdemeanor and traffic cases.

The major trial courts in a state system are called *trial courts of general jurisdiction*. These courts are called district, circuit, common pleas, or superior courts in different states. These courts handle trials in felony cases, but the majority of cases handled by general jurisdiction courts are civil in nature, particularly family law (divorce, custody), probate law (wills), and personal injury. These courts have original jurisdiction.

The term *intermediate court of appeal* is used to describe the state courts of appeal. These courts hear cases on appeal from the lower state courts. Only 39 states have these courts; less populated states do not have a need for them due to a low volume of appeals. In these states, the state supreme court is the only appellate court. The intermediate courts of appeal must hear all appeals that come before them, and most appeals will end at this stage because state supreme courts are highly discretionary when hearing appeals. Intermediate courts of appeal have appellate jurisdiction.

The state supreme courts are the courts of last resort for cases involving violations of state law. These courts have a limited amount of original jurisdiction, but most cases heard by state supreme courts involve appeals from lower courts. As already noted, state supreme courts, like the U.S. Supreme Court, exercise a large amount of discretion when selecting cases to hear. In those states without intermediate courts of appeal, however, the state supreme court must hear all cases that come before it.

Court Actors

A number of individuals make the day-to-day operation of the courts possible. Clerks, bailiffs, probation officers, court reporters, and others provide important functions that are necessary for the efficient functioning of the court system. This section, however, will focus on the major legal players in the courts: prosecutors, defense attorneys, and judges.

Prosecutors

Prosecutors work on behalf of the state and file charges against individuals who violate state law. Prosecutors play a key role in the administration of justice in that they exercise broad discretion in their work. They are responsible for reviewing cases, deciding whether charges are to be filed, and, if so, what those charges will be.

Prosecutors in the federal system take on a wide variety of cases dealing with issues such as computer crime, organized crime, and terrorism. Prosecutions in the federal system are supervised by the U.S. attorney general, who is nominated by the president and confirmed by the Senate. U.S. attorneys, appointed in the same way as the U.S. attorney general, serve under the direction of the attorney general. One U.S. attorney is assigned to each federal judicial district and is supported by numerous assistant U.S. attorneys. United States attorneys are responsible for prosecuting criminal cases involving violations of federal law and litigating civil cases in which the United States is a party.

Unlike in the federal system, prosecutors in state court systems typically handle most of the ordinary street crime that involves violations of state law. Prosecutions at the state level are not necessarily supervised by the state's attorney general; in most states, *state attorneys general* have advisory roles and do not exercise control over prosecutions in the state. State attorneys general are elected by voters in most states.

Chief prosecutors-also called district attorneys, state's attorneys, commonwealth attorneys, county attorneys, or prosecuting attorneys-exercise quite a bit of power in their communities. Typically elected officials (though appointed in a few states), chief prosecutors are the people who make the charging decisions and supervise assistant prosecutors. They are usually the lead prosecutor in high-profile or serious felony cases. Assistant prosecutors, who are typically selected by the chief prosecutor, actually handle most of the cases for the prosecutor's office. They are responsible for the initial stages of a case or lower level felony or misdemeanor cases.

Defense Attorneys

Prosecutors are responsible in some way for all of the cases that come to the attention of the criminal justice system. Defense attorneys, however, do not handle all cases in the criminal justice system. Until the twentieth century, defendants were not given attorneys unless state law explicitly provided them with one (appointed counsel) or unless defendants could afford one themselves. The U.S. Constitution (i.e., the Sixth Amendment) does not guarantee counsel for defendants if they are charged with violations of state law, so individual states have needed to decide if defendants are to receive appointed counsel. In all states, defendants who could pay for their own attorneys could use one, but poor defendants, who constitute a majority of defendants in the criminal justice system, did not have such luxuries.

Because of this, the U.S. Supreme Court handed down a set of decisions that guaranteed appointed counsel to defendants in state cases. Relying on the due process and equal protection clauses of the Fourteenth Amendment, the U.S. Supreme Court, in three historic cases, declared that states must provide appointed counsel to those who cannot afford one. These cases are illustrated in Table 4.2. Even so, the right to appointed counsel is not absolute. For instance, the U.S. Supreme Court does not guarantee an attorney for individuals who do not face incarceration.

Table 4.2 *Provision of Counsel*	
Powell v. Alabama (1932)	the U.S. Supreme Court ruled that states must provide poor defendants with an attorney if they are charged with an offense that carries with it a possible sentence of death
Gideon v. Wainwright (1963)	expanded *Powell v. Alabama*, ruling that states must provide poor defendants with an attorney if defendants are charged with a felony offense
Argersinger v. Hamlin (1972)	continued the trend of *Powell* and *Gideon*, ruling that states must provide an attorney for poor defendants charged with offenses that carry a possible sentence of incarceration (includes some misdemeanors)

Defense attorneys who are compensated by the defendant are called *retained attorneys* and typically work in a law firm or have an established practice. *Appointed attorneys* are compensated by the state and are provided by the state in a number of ways. One type of provision is called the public defender, who provides services exclusively to poor defendants. *Public defenders* are salaried employees of the state and operate within state budgetary guidelines. Public defenders represent about 70 percent of all poor defendants (called indigents) throughout the country, and their services are predominantly found in large and medium-sized cities.

A second type of provision is through *assigned counsel,* which involves private attorneys who provide their services to the court and are compensated for hourly work. Judges maintain a list of volunteers and will select attorneys from the list when services are needed. Assigned counsel systems are more common in smaller cities.

A third type of provision is relatively new. The *contract system* involves private attorneys who bid to provide services in return for a fixed payment. Typically, the state will select the lowest bid in order to contain costs. Because of this, it is believed that contract systems will become a more popular option in the future (Neubauer, 2002).

A fourth type of provision features attorneys who agree to work on behalf of criminal defendants at no cost (or pro bono). These attorneys typically work in private practice and volunteer their time to represent poor defendants. In addition, attorneys who work pro bono may work in conjunction with legal aid societies, which are typically nonprofit organizations that provide services to poor defendants.

The role of the defense attorney is to be an advocate for the defendant, to represent the defendant against the state during the adversarial process. This does not mean doing anything and everything to win, however. Defense attorneys are first and foremost officers of the court and must abide by the rules of the court as well as the rules of the profession when defending a client.

Judges

Judges play an important role in the criminal justice system. A judge is characterized as a neutral, impartial body who will be fair and deliberate in his or her job. It is important to remember, however, that judges are people and are subject to biases like everyone else. Judges must interpret the law, and sometimes a decision by a judge may seem partisan or biased. As long as judges are not engaging in misconduct (e.g., corruption) or succumbing to the effects of age or mental disability, it can be difficult to remove judges from the bench.

The judge has many responsibilities that oversee the functioning of the other players in the system. Judges supervise police procedures by signing warrants and ruling on the admissibility of evidence. Judges interact with defendants by informing them of the charges against them, accepting pleas, setting bail, providing counsel, and sentencing them to a particular punishment. Judges supervise prosecutors and defense attorneys during preliminary hearings and trials to ensure that the rules of the court are followed. Judges interact with juries when providing jury instructions and an explanation of the rule of law. In effect, judges must ensure that the law is being followed and that the law is applied fairly and properly.

The role of the judge in the federal courts and the state courts is similar, but how a person becomes a judge in each system varies. In the federal system, judges are selected by the president and confirmed by the Senate. These judges enjoy life tenure as long as they exhibit good behavior (not committing crimes, not acting in an unethical manner, not becoming too ill to perform). Some states allow for the appointment of judges as well, either by the governor or by the state legislature.

In most states, judges are selected through some sort of election process. Some states allow *partisan elections,* in which a judge's political party is known. Other states use *nonpartisan elections,* in which there is no political affiliation listed. Judges elected by either type of process serve terms of office and must be reelected after a period of time.

Another type of election process is called *merit selection,* in which the governor will appoint a judge to a short term (usually one year), and once that term is up, the voters may elect to retain or remove the judge from office. This gives voters a chance to see what the judge is like, and if voters feel the judge should stay, they will indicate that on the ballot. The judge then serves a specified term of office, and voters indicate retention or removal again once the specified term is finished.

Movement of Cases Through the Court System

Now that the principal players in the system have been identified, it is important to understand how cases move through the court system. In the initial stages of a case, police may ask the court for an arrest warrant, in which a judge will assess the evidence against a suspect and issue a warrant to authorize police to arrest that suspect. Oftentimes, arrests are made without a warrant, and a suspect's case does not enter the court system until first appearance. The U.S. Supreme Court has stated that, after arrest, a defendant must appear before a judge "without unnecessary delay," to ensure that a case can proceed and that police are not abusing their powers by keeping a defendant in detention indefinitely. At first appearance, the assistant prosecutor will provide the judge with the list of charges against a defendant. The judge will then inform the defendant of the charges against him and appoint counsel if necessary. A defendant will make an initial plea and the judge will proceed from there. If a plea of guilty is made, the judge will impose sentence (for misdemeanor cases). Most defendants will plead guilty at this stage. If a plea of not guilty is made, the judge will make a bail decision and set a trial date.

A *bail* decision is made by a judge to ensure that defendants appear for their next court date. In this decision, a judge may or may not require that a monetary figure be paid to the court to ensure that the defendant will return. This figure is typically based on defendants' risk of flight or the seriousness of the charges. For some defendants, a bail amount is not specified, and they are *released on their own recognizance*. This means that the court is fairly certain that a defendant will return for future court dates. For those defendants for whom bail is set, the court will return their money if and when they return to court. If offenders do not return to court, they will forfeit the money paid to the court. In many cases, defendants cannot afford to pay the money necessary to make bail. In such situations, they may enlist the services of a *bond agency*. For a nonrefundable fee (usually 10 percent), a bond agent will post bond to cover the costs of defendants' bail and vouch for defendants' appearance in court.

If a defendant pleads not guilty at first appearance, the next step is usually a *preliminary hearing*. At this hearing, the prosecutor, defense attorney, and judge review the case as it stands to determine if there is enough evidence to proceed. If a judge deems there is enough evidence, the case proceeds toward trial. The next step is formal charging. In some states, a *grand jury* is called to hear the evidence against the defendant and decide if formal charges need to be filed. A grand jury is composed of citizens who will hear the evidence against the defendant to determine if probable cause exists to proceed to trial. In other states, a grand jury may not be used, so the prosecutor is responsible for filing formal charges against the defendant. In these states, the charges are approved by a judge. The formal charging stage is in place to provide a check on the system and to ensure that defendants receive rights they are afforded by law. In the meantime, both the prosecutor and the defense attorney are working on their cases. *Rules of discovery* allow both sides to know the evidence that each possesses, although the rules vary from state to state. Both sides also file motions to the judge. These include motions to suppress evidence, dismiss charges, and postpone the trial date.

If there is probable cause to proceed to trial, formal charges are filed and a grand jury will issue an *indictment* (or a prosecutor will issue an *information*). These formal charges are those that are most supported by the evidence. When this occurs, a defendant is scheduled for an *arraignment,* in which he will enter a plea to the formal charges. Many defendants who have not pleaded guilty already will do so at this stage. For those who plead not guilty, a trial will commence. At this point, a defendant may choose a *bench trial,* in which the judge listens to the evidence and renders a verdict, or a *jury trial,* in which a jury of citizens listens to the evidence and renders a verdict. This is a different group of citizens than those composed to hear evidence in a grand jury. If a jury trial is requested, jury selection begins.

After a jury has been selected, the trial begins. Both the prosecutor and the defense attorney provide opening statements, which give the jury an idea of what each side hopes to demonstrate. Next, the prosecution begins its case, which includes cross-examination of witnesses by the defense. After the prosecution rests, the defense brings its case, which includes cross-examination by the prosecution. After each adversary has presented its side, each provides closing arguments. Next, the judge instructs the jury on the charges, the evidence, and the law and sends them to deliberate. To find a defendant guilty, a unanimous jury must find that the prosecution proved its case beyond a reasonable doubt. *Unanimous* means that all members of the jury find the defendant guilty. A unanimous jury is necessary to find a defendant not guilty as well. If the jury is not unanimous, if even one juror does not agree with the rest, this is called a *hung jury,* and the judge will declare a *mistrial.* This means that the trial is over, but the prosecution has the opportunity to try the defendant again. It is important to remember that in a criminal trial, it is the prosecution's responsibility to prove the defendant guilty of the charges-the defense does not prove that a defendant is innocent. It is the defense's job to provide reasonable doubt; in effect, questioning the prosecution's case just enough so that the burden of proof has not been met.

If a jury has rendered a guilty verdict, a defendant is then sentenced. Except in death penalty cases, it is the judge who sentences the defendant after a jury has found him guilty of the charges against him. In death penalty cases, the jury makes a sentence recommendation, and the judge, who usually follows that recommendation, formally sentences the defendant. After sentencing, the defendant is sent to carry out the sentence in a way that is expressed by the court. A defendant has the right to appeal his conviction or sentence, but most defendants do not appeal their cases.

Current Issues

The court systems across the country are similar in many respects, but each court system is unique due to the various laws, rules, and procedures under which all have to operate. A common theme, however, is overcrowding. Some states have attempted to alleviate this problem by increasing the amount of funding to the more overworked areas, particularly the courts of limited jurisdiction, and creating a centralized court system under the direction of a state administrator. Other jurisdictions have created specialty courts, such as *drug courts,* that handle certain types of cases in order to siphon them out of the primary court system. The use of *juvenile courts* allows for the adjudication of youthful offenders outside the adult criminal justice system.

Another method of keeping cases out of the primary court system is called *alternative dispute resolution.* This involves an informal resolution to problems that may not benefit from ordinary court intervention. The most common form of alternative dispute resolution is called *mediation,* in which a neutral party discusses the problem with the affected parties and attempts to find a feasible solution to the problem. The success of these alternative programs is questionable, however. Steury and Frank (1996) report that although individuals who do participate in these programs are usually pleased with the process and its outcomes, the programs are marked by a large number of no-shows and failures to reach a disposition.

Some court systems are more successful than others when dealing with the overcrowding problem, but many city and urban courts, burdened with an overwhelming caseload, continue to struggle with overworked and underpaid personnel, keeping the assembly-line justice model of case processing alive.

References

Court Statistics Project. (2001). *State court caseload statistics, 2001.* Williamsburg, VA: National Center for State Courts.

Neubauer, D. (2002). *America's courts and the criminal justice system.* Belmont, CA: Wadsworth.

Packer, H. (1968). *The limits of the criminal sanction.* Palo Alto, CA: Stanford University Press.

Steury, E., & Frank, N. (1996). *Criminal court process.* St. Paul, MN: West.

Suggested Readings

Due Process and Crime Control Models of the Criminal Justice System

Packer, H. (1968). *The limits of the criminal sanction.* Palo Alto, CA: Stanford University Press.

Courts and Court Processes

Carp, R., & Stidham, R. (1990). *The judicial process in America.* Washington, DC: Congressional Quarterly Press.

Politics in the Administration of the Court System

Glick, H. (1990). *Courts in American politics: Readings and introductory essays.* New York: McGraw-Hill.

Discussion Questions

1. Since the attacks on the World Trade Center and the Pentagon on September 11, 2001, the criminal justice system has faced unique circumstances with regard to the investigation and prosecution of individuals believed to be involved in terrorism. How would the court system handle individuals who are

suspected of terrorist activity, but have yet to break any laws? In other words, what is the court system's role in balancing the need for national security with the rights of suspects?

2. The provision of counsel for poor defendants has been criticized for the lack of resources allotted by state and local governments, resulting in what some consider ineffective assistance of counsel. What are the problems associated with this lack of resources, and how do these problems affect the other aspects of the criminal justice system (i.e., police and corrections)? ✦

Chapter Five

Corrections

Key Concepts and Terms

- Community Supervision
- Determinate Sentencing
- Diversion Programs
- Indeterminate Sentencing
- Intermediate Sanctions
- Jail
- Net Widening
- Parole
- Prison
- Prison Violence and Coping
- Probation
- Punishment
- Sanctions

Introduction

Punishment for the violation of group norms, rules, and laws is a common element across human history and societies. Social life imposes various restrictions on behavior, and violations of these restrictions and rules carry the possibility of a negative response, whether the response is informally handed out by the head of a household or reflects the official commands of a modern-day court. Punishment may be justified for a variety of social, political, moral, or religious reasons. In ancient times, punishment for a violation of a social norm or law was often handled locally, either by the family, clan, or head of the community. Larger and more organized societies typically used more formal procedures for investigating, prosecuting, adjudicating, and punishing an offender. There was considerable variation in the response, however, depending on the type of law or custom that was violated, who the offender and victim were, the specific geographic location of the incident, and the exact historical time period.

Nearly every society has had some arrangements for the temporary confinement of offenders. Some ancient civilizations, such as Greek and Roman society, also had facilities designed to hold offenders for longer periods of time. In general, however, punishment in premodern Western societies and colonial America primarily involved the use of monetary compensation or corporal punishments. This is not to suggest that imprisonment did not occur, but it was far from the most common or most important form of punishment.

A feature of modern societies is the formal organization and routinization of social tasks and social life. Increasingly controlled and managed, for example, has been the enforcement of laws and punishment of law violators. With the spread of democratic values and market capitalism, however, criticism of the use of physical punishment also increased. Furthermore, existing punishment and facilities of the day were perceived as ineffective and counterproductive. As society shifted from a top-down power structure to one based (theoretically) on the sovereignty of the people, new forms of punishment were needed to reflect these new social relations. It was during this time that the modern-day penitentiary was born. This marked beginning of formal organizational structures designed to carry out punishments (see Morris & Rothman, 1995; Rothman, 1971).

Several major penal institutions were created in the United States between 1790 and 1830. Although there were differences in the design and operation of these early penitentiaries, they were more similar than not. In less than one hundred years, punishment changed from the rather arbitrary use of physical punishment to a model emphasizing the confinement and correction of individual offenders through segregation, regimentation, and control. Offenders were increasingly segregated based upon personal characteristics. As a result, female offenders, juvenile delinquents, and the mentally ill were placed in facilities separate from male adult criminal offenders. By the turn of the twentieth century, state agencies and bureaucracies were being created to carry out the punishments ordered by the courts in a more systematic and consistent manner. For example, in the early twentieth century, probation departments were increasingly created to supervise those offenders given the opportunity to avoid incarceration by abiding by certain conditions while in the community. Even though the story is more complex than the preceding description, the ongoing development of modern criminal justice and corrections should be seen as a function of the changing circumstances, needs, values, and organization of the communities they serve.

Contemporary Corrections

The correctional components of the criminal justice system are generally responsible for carrying out the punishments imposed by a court for a particular offender. The correctional system of a given jurisdiction, however, does not act in an isolated manner. For example, in many jurisdictions, probation officers work either for the judiciary or are an integral part of the judicial process. Probation and parole agents may also work closely with law enforcement in the supervision or apprehension of offenders on community supervision, or both.

This chapter examines the various types of sanctions currently imposed by the courts and the agencies and institutions responsible for those sanctions. It concentrates on broader issues and emphasizes those systems responsible for processing the bulk of offenders facing the criminal justice system each day. This means that it addresses primarily state and local jurisdictions. This overview also discusses contemporary practices in general rather than attempting to identify the various distinctions among jurisdictions. As noted elsewhere, there is a great deal of variation in criminal justice practices within and across jurisdictions.

Though there may be similarities among jurisdictions, each has its own model for organizing a criminal justice system. The federal government has a specific criminal justice system for defendants arrested and prosecuted for violating federal criminal statutes and a correctional system to carry out the punishments ordered by the federal courts. When it comes to violations of state law, the picture becomes more complex, as each state has its own criminal justice system and various subsystems within that larger framework. Defendants convicted of violating state felony statutes and sentenced to prison are generally sent to a facility run by a state correctional agency. Defendants convicted of misdemeanors and sentenced to time in jail are primarily held in a facility funded and run by a city or county government. Responsibility for supervising defendants convicted of violating misdemeanor or felony statutes and sentenced to nonprison sanctions is greatly varied. In some jurisdictions, management of defendants sentenced to community supervision is the responsibility of court employees, but in other jurisdictions, a state agency (such as a department of corrections) handles supervision duties. There are also combination or hybrid models of organizing correctional services, in which the sanction imposed or the jurisdiction determines who will supervise an offender in the community or residential facility.

Punishment in Contemporary America

There have traditionally been several philosophies or justifications for punishment. Which justification is utilized in a given jurisdiction may vary depending on recent social and political forces as well as the circumstances of a particular case. Different types of sanctions are often justified based on different rationales. Some penalties may be viewed as utilitarian in nature with goals such as deterrence, rehabilitation, or incapacitation (Harris, 1992). Some penalties may be perceived to be retributive in the sense that an offender has committed a crime that deserves to be punished without regard to the consequences of that punishment. Though philosophically distinct, in practice, criminal justice sanctions tend to be justified based on a number of rationales. During certain periods of time, however, some justifications garner increasing public and political support.

During the past 25 years, there has been a general trend in the United States and Western European countries to respond to law violators with more severe penalties and decreasing support for rehabilitative efforts toward crime and offenders (Donzinger, 1996; Austin & Irwin, 2001). In the United States, this has resulted in most jurisdictions passing lengthier prison sentences, requiring more punitive sanctions, and attempting to limit the discretion of judges or correctional administrators to reduce sentence lengths. Although these changes apply to a wide variety of behaviors, violent crimes and drug law violations have been particularly affected (Blumstein & Beck, 1999). Perhaps most important has been the increasing effort toward the "war on drugs" that has been fought (with intermittent strength) during the past 30 years. As a consequence, drug law violators now make up a significant percentage of offenders in criminal courts and under correctional supervision (Blumstein & Beck, 1999; Austin & Irwin, 2001).

The results of heightened attention and more punitive responses to crime are indicated in Figure 5.1. Presently, state and federal prisons and local jails hold over 1.9 million offenders. This represents a fourfold increase in the *incarceration rate* (the number of incarcerated persons for every 100,000 persons in the population) in the past 30 years. As a result, the United States has the second highest incarceration rate in the industrialized world (behind Russia) and an extremely high rate compared with Western European countries (Mauer, 1997). There are over 6.5 million persons under some form of correctional

Figure 5.1
Adult Correctional Population Trends in the United States

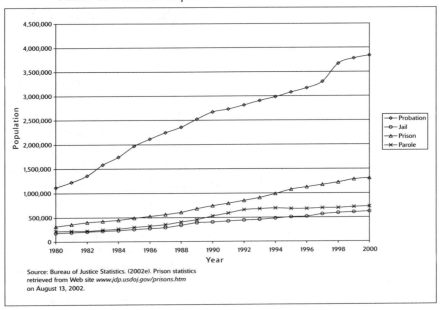

Source: Bureau of Justice Statistics. (2002e). Prison statistics
retrieved from Web site *www.jdp.usdoj.gov/prisons.htm*
on August 13, 2002.

supervision in the United States (Bureau of Justice Statistics, 2002a, 2002b). The populations on probation, parole, and within jails have increased at similar or higher rates than the prison rate. Most interesting is that these changes have occurred during a period that has not seen a dramatic increase in crime rates or the rate of reported drug use (e.g., see Bureau of Justice Statistics, 2002d).

To keep up with the constant flow of offenders into the criminal justice system, jurisdictions have had to increase the funding for various justice agencies. Although the funding for all aspects of the criminal justice system has increased, the increase for correctional spending has been the most dramatic (Bureau of Justice Statistics, 2002e). To reduce prison overcrowding, many states and the federal government have greatly increased the bed space within their prison systems through massive prison construction programs. Across the country, correctional departments have experienced significant increases in their funding, while other social and human service agencies and activities have seen dramatic decreases in their budgets (Blumstein & Beck, 1999).

Sentencing and Sanctions

Sentencing courts in the United States have a variety of sanctions at their disposal, and there is considerable variation across jurisdictions. The term *sanction* is often used interchangeably with punishment and refers to a specific punishment (e.g., fine, probation, prison) imposed by a court. Many jurisdictions incorporate a combination of sentencing types rather than adhering to a "pure model" (Tonry 1999). Furthermore, within the same jurisdiction, the sentencing model for felonies may be different for misdemeanors, and different models may be used for adults and juveniles. However, most jurisdictions' sentencing practices can be described as incorporating one or more of the models discussed. Although many jurisdictions have a variety of punishments for adult offenders, not all jurisdictions will use all of the sanctions discussed.

Lawmakers in each jurisdiction pass criminal statutes that indicate what behaviors are prohibited and what penalties an individual can receive if convicted of that crime. The law typically includes a description of either the maximum sentence (often in terms of incarceration length) or a procedure for determining the appropriate sentence.

Though sentencing practices are often quite complex and generalities are difficult to make given the large number of criminal justice systems in the United States, a jurisdiction's sentencing practices can be described as either following a determinate or indeterminate sentencing model (Reitz, 1998; Tonry, 1999).

Sentencing Models

Determinate sentencing refers to the general practice of sentencing offenders to specific and set periods of correctional supervision (community or institutional) that have been determined by the court. Also referred to as "flat" or "fixed" sentences, determinate sentences result in a defendant knowing exactly how long incarceration will be. This means that, minus good time credits, a defendant given a determinate sentence will serve a sentence length that is reasonably close to that imposed by the court. *Good time credits* are reductions in an inmate's sentence length that are usually awarded for good behavior while incarcerated and can be used in determinate and indeterminate sentencing jurisdictions. Good time credits are awarded at the discretion of correctional staff and administration based on statutory guidelines.

Indeterminate sentencing involves a court sentencing a defendant to a minimum and maximum range of time that the offender will serve. The exact time a prisoner is required to remain under supervision is determined by an evaluation of the prisoner's record and behavior while under supervision. This evaluation is conducted by the jurisdiction's parole board or agents of the parole authority. The *parole board* is a group of persons given the authority to make release and revocation decisions for offenders under some form of correctional supervision in an indeterminate sentencing system. The sentence is considered indeterminate because the exact length of the sentence is not determined until the defendant begins to serve that sentence. After an inmate serves a minimum term (perhaps minus any good time credits), he or she will be eligible for parole release. Simply because inmates are eligible for parole does not mean they will be released. Parole boards often use guidelines to assist them in making consistent decisions in evaluating whether a prisoner should be paroled. If prisoners are released before the end of their maximum sentence length, they are placed on *parole supervision*. This is a form of community supervision that requires them to adhere to certain restrictions and rules in exchange for early release. Some jurisdictions use indeterminate sentences for both sentences to prison and community supervision.

Because the vast majority of criminal defendants are convicted of crimes after pleading guilty or no contest, a sentencing recommendation is often agreed upon by the prosecutor and defense counsel in exchange for a guilty plea. One of the major concerns for defendants convicted of two or more crimes is whether their sentences run consecutively or concurrently. *Consecutive sentences* require that a defendant complete one sentence completely before serving a sentence for the second crime. A *concurrent sentence* means that all of the sentences imposed on a defendant are to run simultaneously. Thus, concurrent sentences result in an actual sentence length that is considerably shorter than consecutive sentences. Another practice is the use of a *split sentence,* in which a defendant is sentenced to a term of incarceration followed by a period of court-ordered community supervision (thus distinguishing it from parole supervision).

Sentencing guidelines are a fairly recent tool used in the sentencing of criminal offenders and are formal guidelines created by a legislative agency or sentencing commission to assist the courts in determining the appropriate sentence for a given offender (Tonry, 1988). Sentencing guidelines, especially those developed by a commission, were increasingly implemented during the 1980s and 1990s as a response to criticisms that state judges and parole boards were too inconsistent in their decisions affecting sentence length (Tonry, 1993). Similarly, federal sentencing guidelines went into effect in 1987. Variations on sentencing guidelines include merely indicating a range of suggested sentences to mandating a specific sentence with relatively little variation.

Although often associated with determinate sentences, sentencing guidelines can be used in indeterminate models as well. The guidelines often use several measures to evaluate the seriousness of the offense and the dangerousness of the offender. Variables (such as the number and type of conviction offense, a measure of the defendant's prior record, and whether the person was under correctional supervision at the time of the offense) may be used to place a defendant within a grid that has a corresponding sentence. In some jurisdictions, judges have a degree of discretion to impose a more or less severe sentence on a defendant if aggravating or mitigating circumstances exist.

Aggravating circumstances are factors associated with the offender or the offense that purportedly merit a more severe penalty. Such circumstances may include a particularly heinous or vicious crime or an offender with an extensive prior record. *Mitigating circumstances* are factors related to the offender or offense that may reduce the offender's culpability. These are not legal excuses or justifications, but merely factors that a prosecutor, jury, or judge may consider when deciding the appropriate sentence for a given defendant. Examples of mitigating circumstances may include the age of the offender (young or elderly), the offender's role in the offense, or other relevant individual characteristics, such as one's mental health history. What constitutes a legally permissible aggravating circumstance is usually determined by statute, but mitigating circumstances are often left to the discretion of judicial decision makers.

Perhaps the key factor in considering the different sentencing models is who has the discretion or authority to affect sentence length and the extent of that discretion. In determinate sentencing, criminal statutes indicate maximum sentences that can be imposed and judges may have considerable discretion to impose a specific sentence. In a jurisdiction with sentencing guidelines, that discretion may be greatly restricted. Prosecutors can dramatically affect a defendant's sentence in determinate models by deciding on which crimes they will charge and ultimately convict defendants (Tonry, 1988). In an indeterminate model, it is primarily the correctional department, through the parole board and recommendations by correctional personnel, that have the greatest discretion in affecting sentence length. The trend during the past 25 years has been to limit judicial and correctional discretion in sentencing (Ditton & Wilson, 1999; Petersilia, 1999). Indeterminate sentencing, however, continues to exist in a large number of American jurisdictions.

Available Sanctions

Jurisdictions vary greatly in the number and types of sanctions that they can use for law violators. Although prison is often the first punishment that comes to mind, it is actually not the most common punishment used for violations of the law. Incarceration in a state correctional institution is typically reserved for the most serious offenders and those who could not abide by the rules of other previously imposed penalties. On a daily basis, courts that deal primarily with misdemeanor crimes handle a far greater volume of offenders than courts that deal exclusively with felony offenders. Even among defendants convicted of felonies, nonprison sanctions are far more common than prison sentences (see Figure 5.1). Generally, the most severe penalties (e.g., imprisonment and the death penalty) are imposed the least, despite popular impressions to the contrary. Imprisonment issues have become increasingly important for a number of reasons, however, including the considerable resources required, the various consequences of incarceration, and its expanding use in the United States (see Figure 5.1).

When sentencing defendants convicted of crimes, courts may use a variety of punishments rather than simply relying on one sanction. It is quite common for offenders to receive a combination of these penalties. Available sanctions for felony offenders include a range of punishments that falls on a continuum based on their severity. Table 5.1 provides a visual representation and description of the range of sanctions that may be found in various jurisdictions in the United States. Although this is not an exhaustive list, it provides a brief overview of some of the more common sanctions for felony offenders.

Table 5.1
Common Felony Sanctions

Probation	A term of supervision in which offenders can remain in the community provided that they follow a set of rules (conditions of probation) in lieu of incarceration. The frequency of contact required between the offender and the probation department will vary depending on the jurisdiction and the offense.
Fines	Fines are often a part of a larger probation sentence. Some jurisdictions have developed more rigorous monetary penalties called "day-fines" that require payment of a percentage of an offender's income over time rather than a flat fee.
Community Service Work (CSW)	CSW requires that a set number of volunteer hours be completed within a specified period of time. Some jurisdictions use CSW as a stand-alone punishment, especially for misdemeanor offenders. CSW for felony offenders is usually a requirement of their probation sentence.
Day Reporting Center (DRC)	This sentence places an offender on a form of community supervision and requires an offender to report to a DRC on a daily or near daily basis. The DRC may house a variety of services and programs that offenders are required to participate in such as drug testing, GED courses, counseling, etc.

(Continued)

(Continued)

Table 5.1
Common Felony Sanctions

Intensive Supervision Probation (ISP)	ISP is a term of supervision that involves more frequent contact (up to several times a week) between the offender and a probation officer and greatly restricts an offender's freedom. Some jurisdictions may require the offender's confinement to his residence when not engaged in approved activities (house arrest) and the use of electronic monitoring devices.
Community Correctional Facilities	This category includes a variety of facilities designed to hold offenders for relatively brief periods of time. The facility may specialize in drug treatment or other programs. It may serve as a work release facility in which offenders go into the community for work or other approved activities but are required to remain in the facility at all other times. It may also serve as halfway house facility for prisoners.
Jail	Offenders who are sentenced by the court to less than a year incarceration usually serve their sentence in a jail or detention center run by the county or municipality. Jail sentences may involve work release provisions or may be followed by a period of community supervision.
Shock Incarceration	Some states give judges or correctional authorities the authority to grant early conditional releases to eligible offenders who have been sentenced to a period of regular incarceration. This release typically follows a brief period of confinement (30-180 days) and is conditional upon the offender remaining on community supervision for a specified time upon release. The brief confinement is intended to "shock" an offender about the consequences of crime and the nature of imprisonment if they violate their community supervision.
Boot Camps	Referred to as shock incarceration programs in some jurisdictions, boot camps are primarily for youthful or younger offenders convicted of nonviolent offenses. These programs involve a brief (less than 6 months) confinement in a secure facility in which inmates go through a period of drill and instruction modeled on basic military training. They rely heavily on the use of physical exercise and instruction in an attempt to instill discipline, self-control, and normative behaviors. Boot camp may be followed by period of community supervision.
Prison	Also referred to as penitentiaries or correctional institutions. Prisons typically hold felony offenders sentenced to incarceration for more than one year. Different prisons will vary on characteristics such as the security level and the types of services and offenders they are designed to accommodate. Prisoners under a sentence of death are typically held on "death row," a wing in a high-security institution in or near where executions are carried out.

Recently, jurisdictions have sought new sentencing options that are less expensive than incarceration, but more punitive and accountable than regular probation. Often referred to as *intermediate sanctions,* they provide an alternative to either traditional probation or prison. Sanctions such as intensive supervision probation, boot camps, and community residential centers are increasingly used for a variety of offenders. Such programs are celebrated as more cost-effective than prison, more restrictive and punitive than regular probation, and as offering a better opportunity for rehabilitative or deterrent effects on offenders. The remaining sections describe several of the more common sanctions used by criminal courts and the major issues associated with their use.

Community Supervision and Intermediate Sanctions

The generic term *community supervision* is often used to refer to any court-ordered sentence that requires a defendant to be supervised while in the community. This includes regular probation, intensive supervision probation (ISP), and other intermediate sanctions. There are some intermediate sanctions that involve residential rather than community supervision. In 2000, approximately 3.8 million adult offenders were under some form of community supervision in the United States (Bureau of Justice Statistics, 2002d). Although the exact number of offenders serving an intermediate sanction is not known, they represent a relatively small percentage of offenders compared with traditional probation.

Another 700,000 offenders in the community are on parole supervision or postrelease supervision (Bureau of Justice Statistics, 2002d). These offenders can be distinguished from those on probation and under community supervision in that parolees are placed on supervision by a correctional agency, rather than being sentenced to a form of supervision by the courts. In practice, parolees and probationers may have many of the same conditions and may even have the same supervising officer in a given jurisdiction. Perhaps the most important distinction is that parolees remain under the jurisdiction of the correctional system, whereas probationers and others on community supervision remain under the legal jurisdiction of the original sentencing court. Violations of the conditions of supervision for either group require that the offender answer to the authority that retains jurisdiction in his or her case.

Offender Responsibilities. Offenders who are placed under some form of community supervision or placed in an intermediate sanction residential program are given a list of conditions that they must abide by in order to remain in good standing with the court and avoid the possibility of receiving a more severe sanction. Often referred to as *conditions of probation* (even though such conditions can be imposed on those sentenced to intermediate sanctions), these lay out the behavioral expectations of offenders while in the community under supervision or while they are in a residential facility. Failure to conform to these rules constitutes a violation of the offender's sentence. This may result in a supervising officer or staff member submitting a report to the court requesting that the offender's conditions be modified or that the person's supervision be revoked and a more severe sanction be given.

Conditions of probation can be divided into standard or special conditions. *Standard conditions* are those rules that all offenders placed on a certain type of supervision must follow. Common examples of standard conditions include obeying all laws, informing a supervising officer of a change in address or work, and not leaving the state without the approval of a supervising officer. *Special conditions* are those that the court imposes based upon the nature of the crime or characteristics of the defendant. These conditions are usually individualized to respond to the needs and risks of a particular defendant. Examples of special conditions include sex offender treatment, substance abuse counseling, working toward the completion of a G.E.D., and the payment of restitution to a crime victim.

Probation violations are violations of probation conditions and are usually distinguished as either a new offense or a technical violation. A *new offense violation* occurs when an offender under supervision commits a new crime. In such a situation, the offender must deal with the appropriate court for the new crime as well as potentially return to the court that originally sentenced him to have the probation violation resolved. *Technical violations* are violations of conditions of probation or supervision that do not involve violations of criminal statutes. These are violations of rules that regular citizens are not required to abide by but have been made a condition of the offender's release to the community, such as abstaining from alcohol use during supervision or attending drug treatment.

How a supervising officer responds to a violation of probation depends on the nature of the violation, the offender, and the officer's perception of the appropriate response. Minor technical violations are typically handled informally with a warning. More serious violations require the officer to consider the nature and context of the violation and the probationer's progress and likelihood of successfully completing supervision, as well as organizational and office dynamics (McCleary, 1992). New offense violations are nearly always reported to the court (especially felonies), as are technical violations that represent a threat to public safety. Prosecutors and judges have considerable discretion in their response to probation violations, but the probation officer's recommendation can play an important role in the final disposition of the case.

Net Widening. Although intermediate sanctions offer the potential to provide more appropriate sanctions to offenders while reducing costs, in practice, scholars have questioned how new sanctions are utilized by the courts. In theory, a number of inmates in prison could be supervised by use of a less expensive intermediate sanction without sacrificing public safety. Similarly, a number of offenders placed on regular probation are better suited to a more restrictive penalty, but without resorting to prison (Morris & Tonry, 1990).

Intermediate sanctions are promoted as achieving a number of often competing goals (Tonry, 1990). These stated goals include decreasing costs, increasing offender accountability and public safety, and increasing rehabilitative effectiveness. One of the major goals of new programs and punishments such as intermediate sanctions is the diversion of offenders from sentences that were considered too severe or expensive for a particular offender. Unfortunately, research indicates that intermediate sanctions are often applied to offenders who would have received a less severe sanction prior to the availability of the intermediate sanction. As a result, some offenders end up receiving a more severe sanction than they originally would have received (if they would have received any) prior to the creation of this new sanction. Furthermore, those targeted offenders who were supposed to receive the new, less severe sanction (and thus be diverted) tend to be sentenced to prison anyway. This is referred to as *net widening*-when a newly created penalty is used to sanction a larger or different population than the one originally intended.

Although some may see net widening as an appropriate increase in the severity of punishment for offenders, this ignores the rationale for intermediate sanctions. Net widening is a problem for several reasons. First, it increases costs rather than decreasing them by placing offenders who would have received a less expensive sanction (generally, the closer the supervision the higher the costs) on a more expensive form of supervision, without similarly diverting prison-bound offenders. Second, because closer supervision programs generally have higher revocation rates for technical violations (Petersilia & Turner, 1993), a percentage of the offenders who could have succeeded under a less restrictive program will end up in prison because they could not follow the rules of the stricter intermediate sanction. This could add to operating costs rather than reduce them. A third major concern is the larger issue of social control. By using new sanctions to impose more severe penalties on offenders, rather than diverting those who do not require a prison sentence, the criminal justice system is expanding its sphere of control over society and the lives of individual members of that society (Cohen, 1985). As noted previously, recent trends have already demonstrated a dramatic increase in the amount of social control that the correctional systems exercise-both in the severity and the numbers of persons under that control-despite no correlating increase in crime.

Officer Responsibilities. In many jurisdictions, officers who supervise offenders in the community perform a range of duties. The two major responsibilities involve conducting investigations and supervising offenders sentenced by the court. The most important investigation conducted by probation officers is the court-ordered presentence investigation. Normally conducted after a defendant has been found guilty through a plea or trial, a presentence investigation is a document that summarizes facts about the offender, the offense, and other relevant information used by the court to determine an appropriate sentence. Typical information includes biographical information about the defendant's education, employment, substance abuse, and criminal history as well as information about the offense and harm caused to any victims. Other investigations conducted by probation and community supervision officers include postsentence investigations that can be ordered if a defendant is sentenced without a presentence investigation. Pre- and postsentence investigations are often used by the agency responsible for supervising the defendant to assist in its evaluation and needs and risk assessment of the offender.

The most important role of a probation officer is to ensure that offenders sentenced to community supervision follow the conditions imposed by the court. Depending on the type of supervision and the jurisdiction, officers may rarely have in-person contact with offenders or they may have regular office, work, or home contacts, or all of these. Officers verify that probationers are attending all required programs, paying all court costs, fees, and restitution, and remaining drug free by conducting drug tests on offenders, though this is not done for all defendants in all jurisdictions.

Probation officers may also be given the responsibility to supervise offenders who have been placed in a diversion program prior to an adjudication of guilt. *Diversion programs* offer the opportunity to temporarily halt the prosecution effort against an offender. If the offender successfully completes the requirements of the program, the prosecutor's office will dismiss the charges. Diversion programs are usually reserved for juveniles, youthful offenders, or first-time offenders. However, those with a previous felony conviction are usually not eligible for participation in diversion programs. Violation of the conditions of the program can result in the prosecutor deciding to proceed with a criminal prosecution against the defendant.

Effectiveness. Research has for several decades questioned the effectiveness of community supervision programs (for reviews see Morgan, 1996; Petersilia, 1997). Research has also failed to demonstrate the effectiveness of newer intermediate sanctions, such as ISP and boot camps (for a review see Tonry & Lynch, 1996). A major issue in evaluating the effectiveness of a program is determining how a program's effectiveness will be measured. Measurements of offenders' behavior while on probation could include the percentage of offenders who successfully complete the program, the rate of new offense violations during supervision, or the rate of new arrests at the end of a follow-up period after the completion of their sentence. It is important to note that how "success" is measured will greatly affect how successful a program appears.

There have been numerous studies measuring the effectiveness of probation and intermediate sanctions. Research results vary considerably regarding the effectiveness of regular probation, depending on the jurisdiction and the exact outcome measure (see Morgan, 1996). In general, research has found that probation is moderately effective at achieving several goals. Morgan's (1996) review of research reported that various studies have indicated that 15 to 50 percent of probationers had "failed" under community supervision. Probationers tend to have a lower failure rate than prison releasees and parolees, though this is not particularly impressive given the high failure rate of these populations. It appears that those on misdemeanor probation have a much higher success rate than offenders placed on probation for felonies, but this could be due to the lower risk of those defendants or the lower level of supervision (Petersilia, 1997).

Research on intermediate sanctions is even more problematic, indicating that the more restrictive requirements of such programs result in a higher rate of technical violations than found among regular probationers (Petersilia & Turner, 1996). The higher technical violation rates mean that offenders who could have "slipped by" on probation are possibly having their intermediate sanctions revoked and being sentenced to prison. In comparing new offense violations, however, regular probationers and those on more restrictive supervision tend to violate their probation at relatively the same rate (Petersilia & Turner, 1996). Research has also found that boot camps do not appear to have any lasting influence on reducing the recidivism of offenders sentenced to such programs (MacKenzie & Souryal, 1994).

Jails

There are over 3,300 jails in the United States (Bureau of Justice Statistics, 2001a). *Jails* and *detention centers* are facilities designed to hold a variety of offenders for a relatively brief period of time, usually for less than one year. The size of a jail will greatly vary depending on the geographic and legal jurisdictions that the facility serves. Although jails in rural areas and small communities may hold relatively few prisoners, the facilities found in America's largest population centers can be quite immense. Counties or municipal governments operate most jails, while some jurisdictions, such as the federal government, have special facilities for their own detainees in certain areas of the country. There has also been a trend for small jurisdictions to combine their smaller jails into a single, regional center that serves several surrounding communities (Stinchcomb & Fox, 1999).

Jails perform several important functions (Frase, 1998). First, jails are where most offenders are housed following arrest. After arrest, a local judge or magistrate will review the offender's charge and flight risk and set a bail amount, order the offender held without bail, or release the offender on his own recognizance (R.O.R.) until his next court date. Second, jails house defendants who have been sentenced to less than one year imprisonment. Some jail sentences are served on weekends, or the offender may be released to the community for work while residing in the jail. Finally, jails may serve as detention centers to temporarily confine a variety of offenders and individuals until their cases are resolved or until authorities from the proper jurisdiction assume custody. Therefore, juvenile and adult, misdemeanor and felony, and state and federal offenders may all be housed briefly in the same facility, though perhaps in different units within that facility.

Although there are exceptions, jails tend to be chaotic environments and face a number of problems (see Frase, 1998; Thompson & Mays, 1991). Jails have historically been the dumping grounds for the poor, deviant, and marginalized individuals in a community (Clear & Cole, 2003). They seem to be continually under pressure from overcrowding, a lack of resources and training, and the influences of local politics. Many individuals processed into the jail are intoxicated or under the influence of behavior-altering substances, highly agitated, suicidal, and/or mentally unstable when they arrive. Jail personnel often do not have adequate information on an arrestee's needs and risks when he is first booked into the facility. This lack of knowledge may lead to otherwise preventable problems. Finally, the continuous movement of prisoners in and out of a jail facility presents logistical and safety challenges to jail staff and administration. For example, jail inmates are frequently moved for court hearings, community service work, and other activities. The high volume of visitors into these facilities can also provide opportunities for violence, smuggling of *contraband* (any prohibited item or substance), and other rule violations.

Prisons and Correctional Institutions

Historically, serious offenders in many societies were temporarily held in a facility for a brief period of time until authorities passed judgment on them and imposed some other punishment. The idea of using imprisonment as a form of punishment, though not without historical precedent, is a relatively modern idea. In particular, the use of large institutions designed to confine offenders sentenced to extended periods of imprisonment is a fairly recent development in the history of punishment. Although felony offenders in the United States are more commonly sentenced to community supervision than imprisonment, prisons are financially and symbolically important forms of punishment. Prisons are also socially and politically important because they are used to house those individuals who are determined to be unresponsive to community supervision, who pose a considerable risk to the community, or who have committed an offense so serious that they deserve to have their freedom taken away for a given period of time. Although prisons are also known as penitentiaries, correctional institutions, and penal institutions, the term prison will be used in this section to reduce confusion.

Prison Types. In American criminal justice systems, only those offenders who have been convicted and sentenced to more than one year of incarceration for a felony offense are generally held in *prisons.* Although many jurisdictions have a juvenile version of a prison system, the majority of prisoners are adults held in state or federal institutions. At any one time, a prison population comprises offenders sentenced for a variety of offenses, as well as those sentenced to prison for probation violations and those returned for violations of their parole. Individual states and the federal government tend to have a number of institutions within their prison systems. Each prison has certain features that make it more suitable for particular types of offenders. Once an inmate is sentenced to prison, personnel from the corrections department usually conduct an initial *classification* review, in which the needs and risk of the offender are evaluated to determine the best placement of that individual within the prison system. Common topics evaluated in this assessment are the danger posed by the prisoner, the length of sentence, any gang affiliation, physical or mental health needs, and whether treatment programs are available and considered important for the prisoner. Based on this assessment, prisoners are sent to an institution that is classified by its security type.

Most American jurisdictions have three to five different types of prisons that are distinguished by their security level. *Super-max prisons* are primarily found in the larger jurisdictions and represent the most restrictive and secure prisons in the country. Because of their extremely high cost of operation and strict limitations on the number of prisoners they can hold, super-max prisons are generally reserved for the most incorrigible and dangerous prisoners in a correctional system. Prisoners in these facilities tend to be continuously confined to their cells except for very brief periods of exercise. Super-max prisons utilize the most sophisticated security systems and most rigorous safety procedures. *Maximum-security prisons* represent the highest level of security in many states. These facilities tend to hold the most violent and disruptive prisoners in those jurisdictions without super-max facilities. Inmate movement within the prison is very restricted by numerous checkpoints and gates. External barriers, such as walled perimeters, several rings of razor-wired fencing, and armed guard towers, are also common. A third classification known as *close security* is used in some jurisdictions and is between a maximum and medium security prison. Such facilities may be used for individuals convicted of violent offenses who do not require a maximum-security setting or disruptive inmates who do not pose as great a physical threat to other inmates or staff. *Medium security* prisons hold a diverse inmate population and can have a variety of architectural styles. Inmates may have some degree of movement within the institution during certain times of the day and participate in a range of activities. However, the specifics of inmate life and the amount of security can vary considerably, even within different prisons of the same jurisdiction. Finally, *minimum-security prisons* represent the most open and least restrictive type of institution. These can house prisoners convicted of nonviolent offenses, those who pose a minimal security risk, or those nearing final release, or all of these. Minimum-security prisons tend to allow the greatest freedom of movement and offer a range of participatory programs and services for inmates.

Some jurisdictions have *specialized prisons* that primarily house inmates with specific characteristics that pose unique challenges to institutions. These facilities offer treatment programs or services that are tailored to meet the needs and risks posed by particular populations. Examples of these institutions include those dedicated to substance abusing prisoners, sex offenders, and mentally handicapped or psychiatric prisoners. Each jurisdiction typically has a facility dedicated to housing prisoners with severe psychological disorders because of the unique problems such inmates present to the operation of an institution.

Female offenders may be held in jails that house both males and females, but prisons are almost exclusively gender-specific. This was not always the case, however. Historically, females, juveniles, and adult male inmates were often housed in the same facility and perhaps even the same cell. Although females make up about 6 percent of all prisoners and less than 15 percent of all offenders under community supervision, in the past decade, females have been one of the fastest growing correctional populations (Bureau of Justice Statistics, 2000). If this trend continues, correctional systems will have to respond to the increasing proportion of female offenders with more designated institutions and additional resources to serve this population.

Another characteristic that can distinguish prisons is whether they are privately operated or managed and staffed by a jurisdiction's own personnel. Historically, it has not been uncommon for some degree of private interest to be involved in the operation of jails and prisons. Since the birth of the modern penitentiary around the turn of the nineteenth century, American correctional systems have had a variety of relationships with private for-profit businesses and nonprofit agencies. Over the past century, however, the funding and operation of most American prisons has been the responsibility of the public sector.

During the push for increasing privatization of government services in the 1980s, American jurisdictions increasingly began to contract out some of their correctional services (Gowdy, 2001; Harding, 1998). To date, treatment services, community service, and smaller residential programs are more commonly privatized than the major prisons. With rising incarceration rates, prison overcrowding, and increasing operating costs during the 1980s, governments were interested in alternatives that could increase the cost-effectiveness of correctional budgets. Though the term *private prison* is often used to indicate a correctional facility that is managed and operated by a private corporation, the privatization of correctional services can take a number of forms. The authority to operate these facilities is granted through a contract awarded by a jurisdiction's government. Considerable debate exists about the validity of incorporating a profit motive in the punishment of offenders (Gowdy, 2001). There are also real questions about whether private prisons are actually more cost-effective and about the quality of services provided at those institutions. Despite this, punishment is a major enterprise and several states have private prisons that are used in conjunction with the state-run institutions. Only time will tell whether privatization becomes a permanent and growing feature of American corrections or becomes a passing trend that is remembered primarily in history books.

Custody and Security Within Institutions. The primary goal of a prison is maintaining custody of inmates within the institution. So central is this need that nearly every decision affecting the operation of a prison must consider the safety and prison control consequences of that decision. Even within the most secure facilities, at any given time, inmates outnumber *correctional officers* (or guards) who supervise the prisoners. This is particularly true of large, lower security facilities.

Secure *custody* of inmates actually involves several components. First, prisons must insure that they are physically secure and can prevent the likelihood of escape and the introduction of contraband into the institution. Second, prison officials want to reduce the occurrence of inmate assaults on staff. Limiting the frequency of inmate-on-inmate violence is another important goal both for the safety of the inmates and the effect such events have on institutional operations. Finally, prison administrators want to secure the efficient functioning of an institution. A number of procedures (such as head counts), activities (such as the feeding, clothing, and bathing of inmates), and work details create a structure to prison life. The smooth operation of these various activities is vital to a manageable environment.

A symbiotic relationship is thought to exist between prisoners, correctional officers, and prison administrators. Though prison personnel have official (and unofficial) mechanisms at their disposal to insure discipline, prisoners can create considerable disruption in the operation of a facility. Therefore, all sides tend to engage in activities and relationships that will maintain the status quo and reduce disruptions to daily life and routines. Clearly, the most destructive and disruptive event is a *prison riot.* Riots represent circumstances in which prison officials lose all but the most basic control over some or all inmates and institutional operations. As a result, staff and inmate safety can be in serious jeopardy, and considerable damage can be done to the physical structure of the institution.

Prison Violence and Prison Discipline. Violence, or at least the threat of violence, is a common concern among both inmates and staff. After all, prisons tend to be filled with individuals who have already demonstrated a willingness to engage in violent or otherwise unlawful acts. Knowledge about violence within prisons is limited by concerns over the validity and reliability of prison records and the limitations of other methodologies used to study *prison violence.* The level and extent of violence will greatly vary from prison to prison and for different prisoners. Particular features of the prison, such as its architectural design, inmate freedom of movement, and group and individual dynamics can affect the level of prison violence (Adams, 1992; Bottoms, 1999). Research suggests that most prisons are not characterized by the systematic and rampant violence often portrayed in the popular media (Bottoms, 1999; Johnson, 2002). Of course, some prisons and prison systems tend to be plagued by higher levels of violence (Bottoms, 1999; Irwin, 1985; Johnson, 2002). But coercion and the threat of violence appear to be more common than actual physical assaults. Coercion may be used by physically dominating some inmates to obtain items such as food, money, personal services, and sexual favors. This threat of violence, including sexual assault, is very real to prisoners. Furthermore, prisoner assaults on staff and other prisoners do occur and can result in serious injury or death. Prisons for females tend to have less explicit violence than those for males, though violence and the threat of violence are clearly a reality in women's prisons as well. Similar to male prisoners, female "convicts" exist within any given institution who are more willing than others to use instrumental violence and cause disruptions within the facility (Johnson, 2002).

Prison officials have a number of tools to deal with violence and other violations of institutional rules. For violations that are criminal offenses, administrators can refer the matter for criminal prosecution. The difficulty, however, in obtaining a conviction in many of these cases, and the logistical problems involved, often discourage such attempts (Jacobs, 1982). A more common response is to use one or more of the sanctions that prison officials have at their discretion. These include the loss of certain privileges such as visitation, solitary confinement (often called segregation) for a period of time, or a change in the inmate's classification status or location (Jacobs, 1982). Prison officials may also have the discretion to reduce an inmate's good-time credit. In jurisdictions with indeterminate sentencing, parole officials will examine an inmate's behavior and may reject a parole application if an inmate has a history of disruptive behavior while incarcerated.

Prison Life, Release, and Reintegration

Prison life can be stressful for both inmates and staff. Research indicates that the unique nature of prison life results in a distinct subculture within prisons. Prison life can be both stressful and monotonous, and adapting to the new environment is essential for an inmate to successfully cope with the demands of prison. Perhaps the most important initial concern is an inmate's personal safety and how to deal with the violence that occurs within an institution.

Prison Subculture and Coping. Most of the research on prison subculture tends to be from the study of maximum-security prisons (e.g., Sykes, 1955). There is reason to believe, however, that elements of a unique prison subculture exist even in less secure facilities. The nature and impact of each prison's culture over its residents varies across prisons and among residents (Bottoms, 1999; Adams, 1992; Johnson, 2002). In an important work, Sykes (1958) identified several characteristics of prison life that contribute to the development of the prison culture and individual responses to imprisonment. These *pains of imprisonment* included the loss of liberty, deprivation of goods and services, the barring of heterosexual relations, limitations to a prisoner's autonomy, and concerns over personal security. These pains are thought to be central features of prison life and require adaptations by individual prisoners if they are to cope in any positive manner (Johnson, 2002). Researchers also believe that individual characteristics will affect a particular prisoner's ability to adjust. The *importation model* suggests that the skills, experiences, and attributes that individuals bring with them into a prison environment affect the prison culture and the ability of an individual to adjust (Adams, 1992). Increasingly, researchers recognize that it is likely that the interaction of an individual's attributes with the unique physical and social dynamics of a given institution will determine the nature of the prison culture and how an individual is able to cope within that setting (Adams, 1992). Whatever the specifics of a given institution's subculture, it is important that a prisoner become socialized into this environment by learning the norms or expectations of behavior and various techniques to cope and adapt.

Prison Programs. With the exception of the highest security prisons, most prisons offer some *prison programs,* promoted as helping with offender rehabilitation and increasing the structure and activities involved in an inmate's daily routine. The number and types of programs vary in different institutions and jurisdictions. In many jurisdictions, inmates can receive good-time credits by productively participating in approved activities. In states with indeterminate sentencing, inmates may consider that participation in certain programs improves their chances of an earlier parole release. Prisoners may be given a particular work assignment that constitutes a major part of their day. Many basic prison operations (such as food service, laundry, and groundskeeping) are carried out by prisoners with varying degrees of staff supervision. Other prison programs may be of a more voluntary nature. Participation in activities such as religious groups, substance abuse and counseling programs, educational classes, and charity and self-help groups may be offered for interested and eligible prisoners. Though the funding for such programs tends to be a relatively low priority, many scholars and practitioners consider these types of activities to be important in helping prisoners cope with the stresses of prison life and in improving a prisoner's likelihood of successful reintegration after release (e.g., Gaes et al., 1999).

Types of Release. Over 90 percent of all prisoners will eventually be released from prison (Petersilia, 1999). This means that a significant number of convicted offenders will need to transition from the highly structured prison environment to the relative freedom of open society. Upon release, most prisoners must identify new ways to meet basic needs (such as food, shelter, employment, and clothing) that were previously provided by the institution. Failure to adequately secure these will decrease the likelihood that a released offender will be able to successfully reintegrate into the community.

Depending on the jurisdiction and the particular inmate, prisoners may be released from prison in several ways. Perhaps the most important distinction is whether the prisoner will be under any form of supervision after release. Prisoners may be sentenced to a split sentence, in which they will serve a period of probation following their release. In determinate sentencing jurisdictions, offenders may be released after an expiration of their sentence and have no supervision following release. In jurisdictions with parole, it is possible that an individual prisoner could be denied parole and be required to serve his or her maximum sentence and would, therefore, have no parole supervision after release. There appears to be a preference, however, to have at least some period of community supervision for prisoners following their release (Petersilia, 1999).

Some jurisdictions with a determinate sentencing model have created a period of supervision for released prisoners called *supervised release* or postrelease supervision. Released prisoners are required to report to a community supervision office located near the place they will reside and are assigned to a supervising officer. Similar to those on probation and parole, prisoners are required to abide by certain conditions following their release to the community. The length of supervision may vary depending on the nature of the crime that the defendant was convicted of or the length of time he or she was incarcerated. A violation of these conditions may result in an offender's return to prison for a period of time.

Prisoners sentenced to an indeterminate prison term may be released by the parole authority after they have served their minimum sentence to *parole supervision*. Prisoners must consent to certain conditions prior to release, and failure to do so will result in a denial of their release. Parolees are assigned to a parole office and officer near the place the prisoner indicates he will reside after release. Parolees are supervised until the expiration of their maximum sentence or until the parole authority terminates their supervision. Failure to comply with the conditions of release may result in a parolee being returned to prison until the parole authority grants a new parole release or until the expiration of his sentence. Although parole boards have often been criticized as being too lenient in their release decisions, it appears that they have recently become more conservative and punitive in their decision making.

Reintegration Challenges. Prisoners face a multitude of problems and challenges that they must overcome if they are to avoid returning to prison. Research indicates that lack of adequate and consistent employment is one of the major characteristics associated with a return to prison (Petersilia, 1999). In addition, offenders may face difficulties because of the "ex-convict" label, a lack of education or eligibility for some jobs, and insufficient life skills for surviving in the modern world. Another major concern is reestablishing family and social networks. Offenders may be estranged from family and friends who could assist with reintegration back into the community. Though not all former associates will have a positive influence on offenders' lives, social isolation can lead to stress and negative behavioral adaptations such as substance abuse and crime.

To reduce the stress and problems of release, many offenders are released into a *halfway house* facility. Such facilities may be privately operated or run by a correctional department. There is considerable diversity in the types of halfway houses. They typically provide inexpensive housing and offer only basic amenities. Prisoners may be placed in these facilities as a condition of their release or may elect to reside there because of a lack of housing options and a shortage of money. More structured facilities may provide a range of services and resources, such as substance abuse counseling, life skills training, or other relevant services, and may place a number of restrictions on residents.

Perhaps the clearest measure of successful reintegration is whether a released prisoner is re-arrested or returns to prison following release. To date, prison has not demonstrated itself as being very effective at preventing offenders (through rehabilitation or deterrence) from future criminal behavior. It is an unfortunate reality that a significant percentage of released prisoners will eventually return to prison. Over 60 percent of released prisoners are re-arrested for serious misdemeanors or felonies within three years of release and about 40 percent of released prisoners return to prison within three years (Petersilia, 1999). There is evidence that prisoners who participate in targeted, problem-specific prison programs have significantly lower recidivism rates upon release (see Gaes et al., 1999). Furthermore, released prisoners who participate in long-term, well-designed, and well-implemented postrelease programs have reduced recidivism. Given spending priorities in American corrections, however, such programs are rare. Moreover, typical programs are often poorly funded and poorly implemented and have demonstrated only limited success (Clear & Dammer, 2003; Gaes et al., 1999; Petersilia, 1999).

Future Issues Facing Corrections

Like all components of the criminal justice system, correctional systems reflect the characteristics and environment of the society that they serve. It is only natural that as society changes, so will the institutions designed to reinforce and protect it. Though there is inadequate space to cover the considerable number of important issues facing corrections in the next few decades, the following discussion will briefly touch on some of these issues.

Perhaps the most compelling issue is what will happen with the prison population and incarceration rate that has seen a fourfold increase over the past 30 years. The war on crime and drugs has taken an enormous toll on government budgets, often to the detriment of other human services, such as education and social services. It is unclear whether jurisdictions can maintain the level of spending on corrections indefinitely or whether public and political support will continue for such expenditures. The wars on crime and drugs have also had a considerable impact on the social fabric of communities and society in general that we are only beginning to understand. Removing such a large number of persons from society will have an observable effect on the children, families, and communities of offenders, likely including a number of negative consequences (Hagan & Dinovitzer, 1999). Expanding the prison population also increases the number of prisoners who will eventually return to the community with additional burdens. What steps are taken to reintegrate this population back into the community and the success of those efforts will be important issues for the country as a whole.

A second major issue is how community and institutional supervision will deal with the *special needs populations* that are increasingly becoming part of the correctional population. One population demanding special attention is the growing number of substance abusers and addicts who are included in the probation caseloads and populations of jails and prisons. Although probation and prisons have always had a disproportionate number of substance (especially alcohol) abusers among their populations, quality drug treatment programs have never been a high priority within correctional budgets. Most programs tend to be understaffed, underfunded, poorly designed and implemented, and simply too short in duration to adequately address the multifaceted problem of substance abuse. The relatively high percentage of HIV-positive inmates presents another set of unique legal, medical, and operational challenges to correctional institutions. The HIV rate in prisons is five times higher than among the general population (Bureau of Justice Statistics, 2001b). How prisons respond to HIV-positive inmates and the measures they take to limit the spread of the virus within the institution will require balancing the needs and rights of the individual with the needs of the other inmates and the institution. Medication and treatment for illnesses related to HIV also increases medical costs for correctional budgets.

A third population that will increasingly become a fixture in institutions and on community supervision is the elderly. As jurisdictions have increased sentence length and decreased the discretion to reduce those sentences, the percentage of older inmates and those on supervision will increase. Incarcerated elderly inmates will require additional medical resources and have special physical and psychological needs. Elderly offenders on community supervision may have fewer financial resources and employment opportunities and smaller social networks on which to rely. The burden that geriatric populations will place on correctional systems is unclear at present, though it is certain that some responses will be necessary to accommodate and address those problems.

Clearly there are additional problems and challenges that correctional systems face. The nature of those problems will be a function of the society that a correctional system serves. The future behavior of other criminal justice agencies, such as the police and courts, will also directly affect what correctional systems do and with whom. Obviously, changes in criminal statutes and penal law will also influence the nature and extent of punishment in the United States. As American correctional systems move into the twenty-first century, it is clear that they will have to deal with a recent legacy that will burden them for some time.

References

Adams, K. (1992). Adjusting to prison life. In M. Tonry (Ed.)., *Crime and justice: A review of research* (pp. 275–360). Chicago: University of Chicago Press.

Austin, J., & Irwin, J. (2001). *Its about time: Americas imprisonment binge.* Belmont, CA: Wadsworth.

Blumstein, A., & Beck, A. (1999). Population growth in U.S. prisons. In M. Tonry and J. Petersilia (Eds.), *Prisons* (pp. 17–62). Chicago: University of Chicago Press.

Bottoms, A. (1999). Interpersonal violence and social order in prisons. In M. Tonry and J. Petersilia (Eds.), *Prisons* (pp. 205–282). Chicago: University of Chicago Press.

Bureau of Justice Statistics. (2000). *Correctional populations in the United States, 1997.* Washington, DC: U.S. Department of Justice.

Bureau of Justice Statistics. (2001a). *Census of jails, 1999.* Retrieved from the Bureau of Justice Statistics Web site, *www.ojp.usdoj.gov/bjs/abstracts/cj99.htm* on August 13, 2002.

Bureau of Justice Statistics. (2001b). *HIV in prisons and jails, 1999.* Retrieved from the Bureau of Justice Statistics Web site, *www.ojp.usdoj.gov/bjs* on August 5, 2002.

Bureau of Justice Statistics. (2002a). *The number of adults in the correctional population has been increasing.* Retrieved from the Bureau of Justice Statistics Web site, *www.ojp.usdoj.gov/bjs/glance/corr2.htm* on August 10, 2002.

Bureau of Justice Statistics. (2002b). *Prisoner statistics.* Retrieved from the Bureau of Justice Statistics Web site, *www.ojp.usdoj.gov/bjs/prison.htm* on August 10, 2002.

Bureau of Justice Statistics. (2002c). *Prison statistics.* Retrieved from the Bureau of Justice Statistics Web site, *www.ojp.usdoj.gov/prisons.htm* on August 13, 2002.

Bureau of Justice Statistics. (2002d). *Probation and parole statistics.* Retrieved from the Bureau of Justice Statistics Web site, *www.ojp.usdoj.gov/bjs/pandp.htm* on August 10, 2002.

Bureau of Justice Statistics. (2002e). *Serious violent crime levels continue to decline in 2000.* Retrieved from the Bureau of Justice Statistics Web site, *www.ojp.usdoj.gov/bjs/glance/cv2.htm* on August 10, 2002.

Clear, T. R., & Cole, G. (2003). *American corrections.* Pacific Grove, CA: Brooks/Cole.

Clear, T. R., & Dammer, H. R. (2003). *The offender in the community.* Belmont, CA: Thomson/Wadsworth.

Cohen, S. (1985). *Visions of social control.* Cambridge, MA: Polity Press.

Ditton, P. M., & Wilson, D. J. (1999). *Truth in sentencing in state prisons.* Washington, DC: Bureau of Justice Statistics.

Donziger, S. R. (Ed.). (1996). *The real war on crime.* New York: HarperPerennial.

Frase, R. S. (1998). Jails. In M. Tonry (Ed.), *The handbook of crime and punishment* (pp. 474–508). New York: Oxford University Press.

Gaes, G. G., Flanagan, T. J., Motiuk, L. L., & Stewart, L. (1999). Adult correctional treatment. In M. Tonry and J. Petersilia (Eds.), *Prisons* (pp. 361–427). Chicago: University of Chicago Press.

Gowdy, V. B. (2001). Should we privatize our prisons: The pros and cons. In E. J. Latessa, A. Holsinger, J. M. Marquart, and J. R. Sorensen (Eds.), *Correctional contexts: Contemporary and classical readings* (pp. 198–208). Los Angeles: Roxbury Publishing.

Hagan, J., & Dinovitzer, R. (1999). Collateral consequences of imprisonment for children, communities, and prisoners. In M. Tonry and J. Petersilia (Eds.), *Prisons* (pp. 121–162). Chicago: University of Chicago Press.

Harding, R. W. (1998). Private prisons. In M. Tonry (Ed.), *The handbook of crime and punishment* (pp. 626–658). New York: Oxford University Press.

Harris, M. K. (1996). The goals of community sanctions. In T. Ellsworth (Ed.), *Contemporary community corrections* (pp. 13–33). Prospect Heights, IL: Waveland Press.

Irwin, J. (1985). *The hail: Managing the underclass in American society.* Berkeley: University of California Press.

Jacobs, J. B. (1982). Sentencing by prison personnel: Good time. *UCLA Law Review, 30,* 217–270.

Johnson, R. (2002). *Hard time: Understanding and reforming the prison.* Belmont, CA: Wadsworth.

MacKenzie, D. L., & Souryal, C. (1994). *Multisite evaluation of shock incarceration.* Washington, DC: National Institute of Justice.

Mauer, M. (1997). *Americans behind bars: U.S. and international use of incarceration, 1995.* Washington, DC: The Sentencing Project.

McCleary, R. (1992). *Dangerous men.* Albany: Harrow and Heston.

Morgan, K. D. (1996). Factors influencing probation outcome: A review of the literature. In T. Ellsworth (Ed.), *Contemporary community corrections* (pp. 327–340). Prospect Heights, IL: Waveland Press.

Morris, N., & Rothman, D. J. (Eds.). (1995). *The Oxford history of the prison.* New York: Oxford.

Morris, N., & Tonry, M. (1990). *Between prison and probation.* New York: Oxford University Press.

Petersilia, J. (1997). Probation in the United States. In M. Tonry (Ed.), *Crime and justice: A review of research* (pp. 149–200). Chicago: University of Chicago Press.

Petersilia, J. (1999). Parole and prisoner reentry in the United States: Adult correctional treatment. In M. Tonry and J. Petersilia (Eds.), *Prisons* (pp. 479–530). Chicago: University of Chicago Press.

Petersilia, J., & Turner, S. (1993, May). *Evaluating intensive supervision probation/parole: Results of a nationwide experiment* (Research in brief: National Institute of Justice). Washington, DC: U.S. Department of Justice.

Reitz, K. R. (1998). Sentencing. In M. Tonry (Ed.), *The handbook of crime and punishment* (pp. 542–562). New York: Oxford University Press.

Rothman, D. (1971). *The discovery of the asylum.* Boston: Little, Brown.

Stinchcomb, J. B., & Fox, V. B. (1999). *Introduction to corrections.* Upper Saddle River, NJ: Prentice Hall.

Sykes, G. (1958). *The society of captives.* Princeton: Princeton University Press.

Thompson, J. A., & Mays, G. L. (Eds.). (1991). *American jails: Public policy issues.* Chicago: Nelson-Hall.

Tonry, M. (1988). Structuring sentencing. In M. Tonry (Ed.), *Crime and justice: A review of research, 10* (pp. 267–337). Chicago: University of Chicago Press.

Tonry, M. (1990). Stated and latent functions of ISP. *Crime and Delinquency, 36,* 174–191.

Tonry, M. (1993). Sentencing commissions and their guidelines. In M. Tonry (Ed.), *Crime and justice: A review of research* (pp. 137–196). Chicago: University of Chicago Press.

Tonry, M. (1999). *The fragmentation of sentencing and corrections in America* (Sentencing and corrections: Issues for the 21st century, No. 1). Washington, DC: U.S. Department of Justice.

Tonry, M., & Lynch, M. (1996). Intermediate sanctions. In M. Tonry (Ed.), *Crime and justice: A review of research* (pp. 99–144). Chicago: University of Chicago Press.

Suggested Readings

History of Punishment

Newman, G. (1983). *The punishment response*. Philadelphia: Lippincot.

Morris, N., & Rothman, D. J. (Eds.). (1995). *The Oxford history of the prison*. New York: Oxford.

Rothman, D. (1971). *The discovery of the asylum*. Boston: Little, Brown.

Prisons and Imprisonment

Johnson, R. (2002). *Hard time: Understanding and reforming the prison*. Belmont, CA: Wadsworth.

Thompson, J. A., & Mays, G. L. (Eds.). (1991). *American jails: Public policy issues*. Chicago: Nelson-Hall.

Tonry, M., & Petersilia, J. (Eds.). (1999). *Prisons* (Crime and justice: A review of research, Vol. 26). Chicago: University of Chicago Press.

Probation, Intermediate Sanctions, and Parole

Abadinsky, H. (1997). *Probation and parole: Theory and practice*. Upper Saddle River, NJ: Prentice Hall.

Bryne, J. M., Lurigio, A. L., & Petersilia, J. (Eds.). (1992). *Smart sentencing: The emergence of intermediate sanctions*. Thousand Oaks, CA: Sage.

Discussion Questions

1. This book has often described the interrelated nature of different elements of the criminal justice system. In particular, the previous chapter has discussed the various roles and responsibilities of the correctional system and its personnel in relationship to other criminal justice system components. Given that situation, what would be some likely consequences for different agencies within the correctional system of a dramatic increase in the number of arrests in a jurisdiction? Identify specific correctional functions that would be affected, how they would be affected, and what might be correctional responses to those changes.

2. Perhaps the major issue facing corrections has been dealing with the dramatic increase in correctional populations during the past 30 years. What do you think would be effective measures to reduce this trend and why would they have such an impact? What do you think are barriers to those policies being implemented? ✦

Chapter Six

The Juvenile Justice System

Key Concepts and Terms

- Adjudication
- Blended Sentencing
- Boot Camps
- Deinstitutionalization
- Delinquency
- Dependent
- Disposition
- Diversion
- Houses of Refuge
- Intake Decision
- Least Restrictive Placement
- *Parens Patriae*
- Reformatories
- Restitution
- Social History Report
- Status Offense
- Transfer or Waiver

Introduction

Dealing with juvenile offenders poses unique problems for society, and an entire system has been established to address juvenile concerns and issues. Where it is possible to talk about a criminal justice system that attempts to coordinate the efforts of the police, courts, and corrections into a functional whole, the juvenile justice system is often viewed as only a tangential appendage to that system. This is largely due to the fact that juvenile justice was founded on a different set of assumptions about the nature of juvenile misbehavior and the proper responses to deal with juvenile transgressors. This chapter will discuss the nature of juvenile misbehavior; the development of the juvenile justice system; the philosophy underlying that system; the role of the police when faced with delinquents, juvenile courts, and corrections; and major topics facing the juvenile justice system.

Defining Delinquency

It is important to note that delinquency did not exist roughly 100 years ago. Until the late 1800s, juveniles were handled in the same fashion as adults and in the same system. As a result, offending juveniles were criminals in the same way as adults who committed an offense. The advent of the juvenile justice system brought with it a new vocabulary, including *delinquency, status offense,* and *juvenile.*

Delinquency can take a variety of different meanings. One way to define delinquency is simply to point to the *criminal law definition* of crime and apply it to juvenile behavior. In other words, a delinquent is any juvenile who violates the criminal code. Thus, a juvenile who commits a robbery, burglary, assault, or any other criminal offense is considered a delinquent. This definition is used throughout the United States. Delinquency is also defined in terms of actions that are illegal only for juveniles. This is usually referred to as a status offense definition. That is, only a person of a certain status can violate the code. Typical status offenses for juveniles include the use of alcohol or tobacco, curfew violations, truancy, disobeying one's parents, or running away. Adults who participate in any of these actions are not subject to sanctions by the criminal or juvenile justice systems. A status offender may be referred to under a variety of different names depending on the jurisdiction. Common terms used are *incorrigible, unruly, dependent, PINS* (person in need of service or supervision), or *CHINS* (child in need of service or supervision). Some of these terms refer to juveniles who have done something wrong or to youths who have been subjected to poor parenting or are victims of a crime and are in need of protection.

In defining delinquency, it is also important to note that the definition of a juvenile (for the purposes of handling a youth in the juvenile system) varies from jurisdiction to jurisdiction. In 37 states and the District of Columbia, a juvenile is anyone under the age of 18. Three states define juveniles as individuals under age 16, and 10 states define juveniles as those under age 17 (Snyder & Sickmund, 1999). Although these ages set an upper limit for juvenile court jurisdiction, many states also set a minimum age for handling youths in the juvenile system. That age is typically between 6 and 10. Besides minimum age provisions, there are often other regulations whereby the juvenile system can retain jurisdiction over an individual who was adjudicated in the system, but has since passed the age of majority. States accomplish this under what are generally known as *youthful offender statutes.* These statutes typically set a maximum age, such as 21, at which time jurisdiction is fully passed to the adult system.

A special set of provisions, which allows for the state to handle juveniles as adults in the criminal justice system, is known as *transfer* or *waiver* provisions. Transfer, or waiver, is a process whereby someone who is legally a juvenile is determined to be beyond the help of the juvenile justice system. Thus, the adult criminal process is called on to handle the youth and protect society. Most jurisdictions set a minimum age at which waiver can be invoked. Traditionally, this has been at age 15 or 16, although there has been a move in recent years to lower the minimum age (often to age 13) or to eliminate a minimum age entirely.

It should be evident that defining delinquency is not a straightforward endeavor. The definition varies greatly based on the age of the youth and the jurisdiction. This situation means that measuring the amount of delinquency can reveal greatly different results depending on how you define the problem. The use of official statistics, particularly arrest data, while a typical source of information, often misses a great deal of juvenile misbehavior due to the minor nature of many juvenile transgressions (such as status offenses). Self-report data, on the other hand, tend to err on the side of recording numerous minor criminal acts and status offenses, but often fail to tap into more serious actions. Exceptions to this problem with self-report data are major efforts such as the *National Youth Survey* and the *Monitoring the Future* project, both of which include serious criminal acts. As previously noted, victimization surveys offer little direct information about offenders and, as a result, are of limited value for measuring the extent of juvenile delinquency.

The Development of the Juvenile Justice System

The history of juvenile justice is a relatively short one. Until the mid-1800s, there was no separate legal status of "juvenile," nor was there a separate system for dealing with youthful offenders; juveniles were treated as either property or little adults. Very young juveniles (particularly under the age of 5) could be bought or sold by the family, just as a cow or other belonging. Once youths turned 5 or 6, they were expected to go to work in the field or a business the same as any adult. Consequently, when youthful individuals violated a law, they were subjected to the same treatment as anyone else. There was no separate system to deal with youthful offenders.

Changes in this status started to appear in the early 1800s as a result of concern over the health and well-being of the poor. The poor were seen as a threat to society, and many communities sought ways to help the poor become productive members of society. A primary response was to take the poor off the streets and provide religious and vocational training. A great deal of attention was placed on dealing with poor children, who were viewed as better suited for the interventions. The earliest institutions set up to address these issues were the *houses of refuge*. The first such institution was established in New York in 1825 and was quickly copied in Boston (1826) and Philadelphia (1828). These institutions handled both adults and juveniles in need of assistance. Unfortunately, the houses of refuge quickly became overcrowded and failed to provide the training and assistance they promised (Pisciotta, 1983).

By the mid-1800s, the houses of refuge gave way to a new set of institutions, the *reformatories*. Although the basic goal of the reformatories was the same as the houses of refuge, they differed in two important ways. First, they handled only youths. Adults were no longer housed with the juveniles. Second, the reformatories typically appeared as a series of small cottages, each of which had a set of surrogate parents and housed a small number of youths. This was supposed to resemble a family setting in which the parents would provide the love and care needed by the children. Unfortunately, the reformatories suffered from many of the same problems as the houses of refuge (Pisciotta 1983). What makes them important is the fact that they started to recognize the unique needs and issues surrounding the young people in society.

Throughout the development of these new institutions, there remained a single system for dealing with criminal behavior by individuals of all ages in society. The failure of the houses of refuge, the reformatories, and similar institutions to deal with problem youths led to the development of the juvenile court. The first recognized individual juvenile court was established in Cook County (Chicago), Illinois, in 1899. The juvenile court was founded on the belief that juveniles needed assistance to overcome the disadvantages they faced in society and that they could be reformed through a system of benevolence, rather than one that punished problematic behavior. The new juvenile court had jurisdiction over all youths aged 15 and younger, no matter what the issue. The court was also supposed to operate in a very informal manner and avoid any resemblance to the adult court. Specifically, due process, attorneys, juries, and other elements of the adult system were excluded from the new juvenile system. The juvenile court was supposed to approach juveniles in a very paternalistic manner and offer them help and assistance just like that found in a family. Another important part of the court was the reliance on probation, rather than incarceration, for problem youths. The actual procedures and workings of the juvenile court generally reflected the character of the different judges and individuals working in the court.

The Philosophy of the System

The new juvenile court conformed to a philosophy that was diametrically opposed to the existing tenets of the adult criminal system. Rather than assume that people acted out of free will and chose to commit criminal and antisocial acts, the juvenile system took the stand that youths were incapable of forming the intent to commit criminal acts. Instead, their deviant behavior was the result of forces that were beyond the control of the youths, or the youths were simply too immature to understand the consequences of their behavior. As such, a strict legal response to juvenile misbehavior, which would include concerns over the constitutional rights of youths, the need to prove guilt and require punishing the guilty, would be inappropriate. The appropriate alternative response would be to nurture, protect, and train the youths so that they could make decisions and avoid problems. This philosophy is known as *parens patriae.*

Parens patriae, or the state as parent, grew out of the English *Chancery Court,* which was tasked with looking after the property rights of orphaned children (among other things). The new juvenile court adopted this philosophy as the guiding force for its operations. The court was to act as a parent to those juveniles who were in need of assistance. *Parens patriae* opened the door to increased involvement in the lives of juveniles and their families. This is probably best exemplified in the passage of statutes specifically outlining status offenses. For example, the original Illinois statute establishing the juvenile court addressed criminal activity, dependency, and neglect. By 1903, however, the state added incorrigibility, curfews, and other status offenses to the court's mandate.

The *parens patriae* philosophy was not new to the juvenile court. Indeed, it was used in an early court case in which a young girl was incarcerated against the wishes of her father. In *Ex parte Crouse* (1838), the mother of a girl asked the court to incarcerate her daughter because the mother was incapable of taking care of her. The father objected and argued it was illegal to incarcerate a child without the benefit of a trial. The Pennsylvania Supreme Court, however, rejected the father's argument, stating that when a parent is incapable of doing his job (or refuses to do it appropriately), the state has a duty, under *parens patriae,* to step in and take action for the betterment of both the juvenile and the community. More important, the court noted that the rights of the parents are superceded by the rights and interests of society. This stance was reaffirmed after the initiation of the juvenile court in *Commonwealth v. Fisher* (1905). In this case, the Pennsylvania Supreme Court noted that when the objective of the state is not to punish or simply restrain a youth, but rather to provide care and protection, the state has a right and duty to step in and take custody of a youth. In essence, if the intent is to help the youth, *parens patriae* allows the juvenile court wide latitude to intervene in the life of the youth and the family.

The *parens patriae* philosophy remained the dominant view in the juvenile justice system throughout the twentieth century. Indeed, it was not until 1966 that the philosophy was seriously questioned in the case *Kent v. U.S.* Though the U.S. Supreme Court did not rule specifically on the philosophy of the juvenile justice system, Justice Abe Fortas argued thatthere may be grounds for concern that the child receives the worst of both worlds: that he gets neither the protections accorded to adults nor the solicitous care and regenerative treatment postulated for children. (*Kent v. U.S.*, 1966)

Justice Fortas was suggesting that the philosophy was allowing the juvenile court unfettered involvement into the lives of juveniles without granting any due process rights to the juveniles, despite the fact that the court was also failing to provide the help and care that the philosophy mandates. Changes in the juvenile justice system over the last 30 years show a gradual diminution of *parens patriae* in juvenile proceedings.

The Police and Juveniles

The role of the police in the juvenile justice system is an interesting one. At first glance, the two organizations appear to be working in conflict with one another. Most people (and the police themselves) view the police as a tool for arresting law violators, gathering evidence to be used in prosecutions, and deterring crime, while the juvenile system is interested in identifying youths who are in need of help and providing an appropriate intervention to eliminate the causes of the youths' problems. The bulk of police work with juveniles does not entail arrest or investigation. Instead, the police invoke their order maintenance role in most interactions with youths. This is especially true when one considers that most juvenile misbehavior falls into the realm of minor property offenses and status offenses.

Much of the training police receive is not applicable to situations involving juveniles. Procedures for arrest, interrogation, searches, and other common police activities are not applicable in many encounters with youths. For example, simply reading a juvenile his rights is not enough to ensure that any statements the juvenile makes will be useable in the future. The officer must consider factors such as the age, maturity, and experience of the youths, as well as the relative power differential between the officer and the youth (both in age and soci-

etal roles), in determining whether the youth is able to freely waive
his rights. Many jurisdictions take a position that no youth can waive
his rights without first consulting with a parent or guardian or an attorney.

If the police decide to take a juvenile into custody, there are specific requirements that must be met. First, youths cannot be mixed
with adults in the same facility. They must be held in a location that
physically keeps them separated from adults. This includes not only
separate rooms or cells, but also a situation in which adults and juveniles cannot see or hear one another. The ideal case is one wherein
the jurisdiction has a totally separate facility or location for handling
juvenile matters. Most often this is referred to as a *detention* facility,
not a jail. Detention facilities can be either secure (locked) or
nonsecure and, in either case, typically do not use bars or other trappings found in adult jails.

The police are also faced with a different set of guidelines when
processing youths they have taken into custody. Generally, there are
restrictions on fingerprinting and photographing juveniles. The traditional rule has been that juveniles cannot be fingerprinted or photo-
graphed, except in circumstances where the identity of the youth
needs to be established. Many jurisdictions have required the police
to obtain permission from the court before taking these actions, and
they must destroy the fingerprints and photographs once they are no
longer necessary for identifying the youth or for use in the immediate
case. Even though this restriction still exists in most places, many jurisdictions have established exceptions that allow for the fingerprinting
and photographing of youths who commit serious adult crimes or
who are repeat offenders. The statutes outlining these exceptions,
however, lay forth very strict guidelines for the use and archiving of
the material.

Most contacts between juveniles and the police are for noncrimi-
nal activity. An entire set of rules and regulations guides what police
can and cannot do with juveniles, and this often results in the police
finding alternative methods for handling youths. One response is
using discretion to simply ignore much juvenile misbehavior. Indeed,
some state statutes specifically authorize the police to use discretion
with juvenile offenders (e.g., Alabama). This is in contrast with adult
criminal codes that typically assume full enforcement of the law. It is
not surprising that the police would ignore a great deal of minor misconduct given the different rules and regulations they must follow

when handling juveniles. Another response by police departments has been to establish separate units that are specially trained to deal with problem youths. These units have specialized functions within the police department. In some places, officers who take a juvenile into custody will simply transport the youth to the juvenile bureau for processing. The officers in the unit are provided special training in dealing with youths and their families, and they have access to the appropriate facilities and resources for juveniles.

The role of the police in juvenile justice remains uncertain. The fact that the police are trained to deal more with criminal offenses by making arrests and building cases for prosecution puts them at odds with the basic philosophy of the juvenile court. The juvenile system is supposed to focus on identifying youths in need of assistance, finding the appropriate help, and aiding in improving the welfare and behavior of youths. Added to this is the fact that most juvenile misconduct revolves around status offenses, victimless crimes, and minor offenses. It is no wonder that the police find themselves in a unique situation when faced with juvenile "offenders."

The Juvenile Court

Most youths come to the juvenile court by way of the police. In any given year, the police refer roughly 85 percent of the juveniles appearing in juvenile court. The remaining 15 percent are referred to the court by parents, schools, or other agencies or individuals (Butts et al. 1994). No matter how youths reach the court, the process and decision points are the same. In general, there are five key stages in juvenile court processing: the detention decision, intake, transfer (or waiver), adjudication, and disposition.

Detention

The initial decision to be made by juvenile court personnel is whether to hold a youth in custody or allow the youth to go home until further action is taken. A *detention decision* is the counterpart to the bail decision in adult court. An adult bail decision considers whether the individual will appear at a later date and whether the person is a threat to others, but the detention decision also considers whether the juvenile is in danger. That is, detention is considered for the good of society *and* the good of the juvenile. Detention decisions are initially made by probation officers or special detention workers, although the final decision on whether to continue detention is up to the juvenile court judge. Most state laws require that a detention hearing be held within a specified period of time, typically 36 or 48 hours. A key concern is whether detention should be used to hold youths who are at high risk for committing further offenses, even in the event that no imminent danger to another person can be demonstrated (Rossum et al., 1987). Critics of detaining youths for this reason generally claim that many youths who are held do not really constitute a threat and, therefore, the detention is a violation of their rights. Such preventive detention, however, has been declared constitutional by the U.S. Supreme Court (*Schall v. Martin,* 1984). Only about 20 percent of the youths brought to the attention of the court are held in detention. The remaining youths are released to their families.

As noted earlier, detaining a youth is not the same as detaining an adult. Juveniles simply cannot be locked into a cell to await their court date. Instead, certain conditions need to be met. Besides isolating youths from adults and providing food and a place to sleep, detention is required to attend to the other needs of juveniles. This includes providing adequate health care, addressing educational needs (particularly if it is during the normal school year), and involving youths in treatment programs. Both the educational and treatment components respond to the *parens patriae* doctrine of helping the youths rather than punishing them. It is not unusual, therefore, for detention centers to hold school classes during the week (often using assignments sent by the juveniles' schools) and to offer some form of treatment programming. These activities are especially important if the youths spend a prolonged period of time in detention prior to a final court disposition.

Because of the relatively short periods that most youths spend in detention, the treatment interventions are often very simplistic and do not address the underlying needs of the youths. Instead, the interventions tend to address the need to keep order in the institution. A very common form of detention programming is referred to as *"boob tube" therapy* (Silberman, 1978). This is nothing more than parking youths in front of televisions all day long. Another common intervention used in detention facilities is the implementation of *token economies.* Under this approach, youths receive points or tokens for acting appropriately and lose them for inappropriate behaviors. The tokens are good toward extra privileges or purchases from a store or vending machine. Other interventions, such as counseling and vocational training, may appear in some facilities, but are not very common due to the relatively short stay for many youths.

The Intake Decision

The second major decision point in the juvenile court is intake. The *intake decision* is the juvenile system's counterpart to filing charges or a grand jury indictment in the adult system. It is at intake that the decision is made to file a *petition* with the court to hear the case or to handle the youth in another way. The petition alleges that a child is either delinquent, neglected, abused, incorrigible, dependent, or otherwise in need of court intervention. This decision to file a petition is typically made by a probation officer or an intake officer. The decision usually comes after the probation or intake officer has reviewed the facts of the case, met with and talked to the youth and his family, gathered background information about the youth (including prior offending, school records, etc.), and considered other alternatives to formal court processing. In recent years, many jurisdictions have begun to mandate that all decisions to file or deny a petition be reviewed by a prosecutor in order to ensure that there is legal standing for the court to take action and guarantee that serious juvenile offenders are not moved out of the system. Despite the move to include prosecutorial oversight, nearly half of all juvenile cases reaching the intake stage are *not* petitioned to the court (Sickmund, 1997).

Youths who are not petitioned to court are not simply let go by intake. Some form of *informal adjustment* is typically mandated by the intake or probation office. An informal adjustment means that the youth will be required to participate in something short of a court procedure. This may be as simple as making restitution to a store for a theft or a homeowner for vandalism, or it could be as involved as attending a series of counseling or treatment programs. It is not unusual for such informal adjustments to require the participation of the parents and other family members, especially if counseling or treatment is mandated. These informal adjustments are an important part of the juvenile justice system and clearly fit the *parens patriae* philosophy of the court.

The Transfer (or Waiver) Decision

One possible option available to the juvenile court when faced with a serious juvenile offender is to *transfer* or *waiver* the youth for processing to the adult system. This is an important decision, because the transfer means that the youth will be subjected to both the due process concerns of the adult court and the same penalties imposed on adult offenders. In essence, the youth will be dealt with as any other adult and will incur an adult criminal record if convicted. A criminal record may have serious ramifications for future employment opportunities, whereas a juvenile record is typically confidential and not subject to later disclosure.

Although the traditional and most common method for waiving a juvenile was to petition the juvenile court to pass jurisdiction over to the adult court, today there are several different types of waiver (Sickmund, 1997). *Judicial waiver,* the traditional approach, is typically made at a hearing analogous to a preliminary hearing in adult court. At this hearing, the prosecutor asks the juvenile court judge to transfer the youth to the adult court for processing. The prosecutor must show probable cause that the juvenile committed the alleged offense. He must also convince the judge that the youth is not amenable to treatment in the juvenile system. What this means is that the juvenile justice system is not capable of helping the youth. This is typically demonstrated through past failures of the juvenile system to correct a problem or the particularly heinous nature of the offense. Basically, the juvenile system must show that the youth is beyond its capacity to help.

Concern over the increasing number and seriousness of juvenile crimes, particularly since 1990, has led to a greater reliance on two other types of transfer: prosecutorial waiver and legislative waiver. *Prosecutorial waiver* refers to the ability of prosecutors to decide in which court (juvenile or adult) to file charges. That is, the prosecutor can use discretion to take the youth straight to the adult court by filing charges at that level. The prosecution is not totally free to make such a decision and is generally bound by state statutes that outline which offenses and which circumstances can be used to send a juvenile to the adult system. The statute, however, does not mandate transfer of the case to adult court. Rather, the prosecutor can choose to keep the case in juvenile court. The last form of transfer is referred to as *legislative waiver* or *statutory exclusion*. Legislative waiver means that the state legislature has determined that certain offenses or circumstances warrant invoking the adult criminal process and mandates that the case be heard in the adult court (Sickmund 1994). The case is excluded from juvenile court processing by statute. The typical cases addressed by legislative waiver are serious personal offenses, such as murder or serious repeat offenders.

Only a small portion of all youths are transferred to adult court; however, a significant number of youths find themselves facing adult sanctions. In 1997, less than 1 percent of all juveniles petitioned to court were transferred to the adult court. This represents approximately 8,400 cases. The number of cases waived to the adult court increased greatly in the mid- to late 1980s and early 1990s, largely due to increases in the number of homicides and assaults related to the growth of crack cocaine use. Recent reductions in the number of waivers, however, have not matched the increases in the early 1990s, and the number of youths waived still exceeds that seen in the late 1980s.

Adjudication

Actual hearings in the juvenile court are referred to as the *adjudication* stage. During adjudication the judge must determine whether there is enough evidence to support the petition and what remedy to use with the juvenile. This is comparable to the finding of guilt and sentencing in the adult court.

The adjudication stage in the juvenile court is supposed to look different from what is seen in an adult court. Under *parens patriae,* there is not supposed to be a determination of guilt. The actual fact that a crime may have been committed is secondary to the needs of youths and their families. Due process considerations of the admissibility of evidence, the use of hearsay evidence, the presence of attorneys, and similar issues are secondary to determining what is in the best interests of children. The entire setting of a juvenile courtroom is often configured to suggest a nonadversarial proceeding. Many hearings are held around a large conference table and the judge does not even wear judicial robes. It is common for the judge to ask all the questions and for the probation or intake officers to offer most of the evidence.

This ideal process of a juvenile procedure has undergone several changes over the past 30 years. Today, there is a greater emphasis on procedural rights in many cases, particularly those dealing with serious offenses (Feld, 1993). Defense attorneys are more prevalent in juvenile proceedings (although still not present in a majority of cases), and determining guilt is more common. Because of the increasing seriousness of many juvenile offenses, many courts have also adopted the trappings of adult court, with a judge's bench, judicial robes, defense and prosecution tables, and concern for due process rights of the youth.

Disposition

Once the court has determined that the facts of the petition are sufficiently supported, a *disposition* (the equivalent to a sentence in an adult court) is determined. Most often the disposition reflects the *parens patriae* philosophy and seeks interventions and treatments that address the needs of the youth and the family. The judge pays a great deal of attention to the recommendations of the probation officers, social workers, psychologists, and others who have examined the youth. Counseling, educational programming, and treatment programs dominate most dispositions, and most of the time there is a strong desire to send the youth home for treatment within the community. Indeed, the vast majority of youths are placed on some form of probation.

However, many jurisdictions have moved to more punitive sanctions in recent years (Feld, 1993; Torbet et al., 1996). This trend has been mandated in many places by legislative attempts to "get tough" on juvenile offenders by setting minimum sanctions that the juvenile courts must impose for some crimes. It is not unusual for jurisdictions to impose these harsher dispositions on older youths who have been involved in repeat offenses. A concern is that these youths will continue their offending once they become adults and are no longer under the juvenile court's jurisdiction. Indeed, many jurisdictions have developed a system of *blended sentencing* as a means of addressing the loss of jurisdiction by the juvenile court before a youth can be adjudicated or before treatment can be completed. Under blended sentencing, the court imposes a disposition, which relies on both the juvenile and adult systems. For example, a 17-year-old who is adjudicated in juvenile court may begin his disposition in a juvenile facility. Instead of simply releasing the individual when he turns 18, the individual automatically transfers to an adult facility and supervision by the adult court. Another possibility is for the 17-year-old to be sent directly to adult supervision from the juvenile court. The opposite can also occur. A youthful adult offender (say age 19) may be found guilty of a crime in adult court, but the court may believe the offender would be better served in a facility or program run by the juvenile court and send the individual to the juvenile system for help. Such blended sentencing is becoming more commonplace as society grapples with offenders who do not quite fit into one or the other system.

Due Process for Juveniles

Starting in the 1960s, challenges to the *parens patriae* philosophy began to have an impact on providing due process protections to youths. Today, youths are afforded some of the constitutional rights that adults have when facing the criminal justice system. At the same time, the courts still recognize the *parens patriae* doctrine as the driving force when dealing with juveniles and have been reluctant to award full constitutional protections to youths in the juvenile justice system. This section touches on some well-known and influential cases that have increased due process protections for juveniles.

As previously noted, the first case to seriously question the *parens patriae* doctrine and the lack of due process rights for juveniles was *Kent v. U.S.* (1966). In *Kent,* the U.S. Supreme Court was asked to examine the rights of a juvenile faced with transfer to the adult court. Kent was a 16-year-old male accused of rape, who had been waived to the adult court without benefit of a hearing, the assistance of counsel, or an explanation of why he had been waived. The Supreme Court decided the juvenile court judge had erred. Specifically, the court should have allowed Kent's attorney to review the evidence and be present at a hearing in order to refute the evidence and offer a counterargument to the court. The denial of counsel was a violation of Kent's Sixth Amendment rights. Further, the Supreme Court ruled that a judge needs to set forth in writing the specific reasons why a transfer is being made to an adult court.

The *Kent* case is important for two reasons. First, it outlined the procedure by which transfer decisions must be made. No such procedure existed prior to that time. Second, and most important, the case established some due process protections for the first time in juvenile procedures. Although the protections applied only to transfer decisions, they opened the way for further challenges to *parens patriae*.

The year after the *Kent* decision, the U.S. Supreme Court ruled in the case *In re Gault* (1967). In this case, a 15-year-old youth was accused of making obscene phone calls and was subsequently sentenced to the state training school until he became an adult. In essence, Gault was given a six-year sentence for a crime that, for an adult, could only bring a $50 fine and two months in jail. The appeal, however, was not over the sentence. Instead, the questions raised dealt with the procedure followed when imposing the sentence. Gault was taken into custody by the police without any notice given to his mother. He was detained until his hearing one week later, at which time he was denied the right to counsel. Moreover, no specific charges were ever filed, the person making the accusation was not required to appear, and no transcripts of the proceedings were kept. The Supreme Court ruled that when there is a possibility of confinement, a juvenile does have certain rights, including the right to an attorney, the right to know the charges against him, the right to confront his accuser, and the right to remain silent (*In re Gault*, 1967). The Court specifically noted that the inclusion of due process rights in juvenile court would not hinder the court's ability to act in the best interests of the child.

The rights of juveniles to due process were further enhanced in 1970 in the case *In re Winship*. In this case, a 12-year-old boy was confined to the state training facility for allegedly stealing $112 from a lady's purse. During the juvenile court hearing, the court adjudicated the youth delinquent using a "preponderance of evidence" criterion. The appeal dealt with whether this standard of proof was sufficient for incarcerating a juvenile. The U.S. Supreme Court noted that the higher standard of "beyond a reasonable doubt" as used in the adult court must also be used in juvenile proceedings when there is the possibility of committing a youth to a locked facility (*In re Winship*, 1970). The Court also questioned the use of the preponderance of evidence, based on its lack of accuracy and openness to interpretation. Each of these cases extended due process protections to a larger number of situations and juveniles.

Despite the growth of due process considerations in juvenile court, some constitutional rights afforded to adults are not applicable to juveniles or the juvenile court. This was made evident only one year after *Winship* in the case *McKeiver v. Pennsylvania* (1971). In this case, the juvenile was denied the right to a jury trial and appealed to the U.S. Supreme Court for relief. The Supreme Court, however, sided with the lower courts and ruled that juveniles were not constitutionally entitled to a jury trial. It did this for several reasons. First, the Court ruled that there is no need for a jury trial to ensure fairness. Bench trials are just as capable of ensuring fairness as a jury trial. Second, the Court did not want to turn the juvenile courts into an adversarial setting, and a jury trial would be much more adversarial. Third, the Court pointed out that the juvenile court was capable of fulfilling its mandate without giving full due process rights to juveniles. Finally, though it did not mandate jury trials in juvenile cases, the Court did note that a jurisdiction could allow for juries if it desired to do so (*McKeiver v. Pennsylvania,* 1971). To a large extent, the court was attempting to balance the move toward due process with the *parens patriae* philosophy of the juvenile court.

These four cases are typically considered the most important cases for the juvenile justice system. They opened the door to review of the actions of the juvenile court and offered some constitutional protections to youths. At the same time, they limited the extent of those constitutional rights and reaffirmed the basic philosophical mandate underlying the juvenile system. Since these cases were decided, many other challenges have been mounted on behalf of juveniles. Some of those cases further refine the rights of juveniles in the juvenile and criminal justice systems. Other cases address larger constitutional issues, such as juveniles' rights to free speech, privacy rights in schools, abortion rights, and many others. Throughout these cases there is an attempt to balance the rights of juveniles as individuals and citizens, with the family and societal needs to protect and raise children to be law-abiding citizens.

Juvenile Corrections

Juvenile corrections take a variety of forms, ranging from institutional and residential settings to probation and community-based alternatives. The primary goal throughout juvenile corrections is to help youths overcome problems leading to misbehavior. The history of many correctional initiatives today dates back to founding principles of the juvenile system. The early houses of refuge and reformatories set the stage for today's residential institutions, and probation has been a cornerstone of dealing with juveniles since before the first juvenile court was established. Before turning to specific correctional interventions, it is important to briefly discuss an idea that seeks to circumvent system involvement altogether: diversion.

Diversion

The juvenile justice system and *parens patriae* are premised on the idea of identifying youths who are in need of help and intervening to provide the needed assistance. However, a major movement in the 1960s, 1970s, and 1980s sought to limit the number of youths handled by the system. That movement was known as *diversion*. The basic premise of diversion was that system involvement could lead to more, rather than less, crime (President's Commission, 1967). That is, the system was *criminogenic*. This position was based on the ideas of labeling theory, which claimed that system involvement tagged the individual as bad, and the individual would act accordingly. Diversion can take place at various points of system contact, including the police sending the child home at the outset without police taking any formal action, mandating informal counseling at intake, and deferring adjudication pending the completion of an early court intervention program. In every case, the idea was to remove juveniles from the system as early as possible.

Diversion was not a new idea. Only the name was new. The entire juvenile system had been premised upon the idea of diverting juveniles away from the adult system. Every new intervention and treatment sought to divert youths to something that was perceived as more effective. Diversion in the 1970s simply meant trying to divert youths from the formal juvenile justice system. This new idea led to the development of many new programs containing the word *diversion* in their titles. In reality, most of the new interventions were nothing more than repackaged, renamed versions of existing programs. Most of these entailed counseling of one form or another. Not surprisingly, therefore, evaluation of the new diversion programs failed to show any great impact on recidivism or the number of youths in the system. Instead, the number of youths under some form of supervision, whether the formal system or diversion programming, actually grew, resulting in what is known as *net widening*. That is, as diversion opened up new alternatives for handling youths, a wider net was thrown to bring in youths who previously would have been left alone altogether.

Institutional and Residential Interventions

The equivalent of adult prisons in the juvenile system is *state training schools*. Youths considered a risk to themselves and the community and beyond the help of community-based interventions are sent by the court to training schools for help. The actual setup of training schools varies greatly from place to place. Some training schools closely resemble adult prisons, with high walls, fences, barbed wire, locked cells, and heavily regimented activities. At the other extreme are training schools built on the cottage design of the early reformatories. These institutions may be totally open, meaning that there are no fences or locked doors to keep juveniles from escaping. The correctional officers in these facilities may actually act more like parents than jailers. The most important part of training schools is the degree of programming that is supposed to take place. Not all training schools are huge institutions located in a centralized location. Today, many institutions resemble the basic ideas of a training school, but are much smaller and are much closer to the homes of the youths they serve. Indeed, even detention centers that house postadjudicated, long-term youths mirror many aspects of training schools.

Most training schools offer some combination of academic education, vocational training, and behavior modification. As in detention, the youths must attend school during the academic year, just as any other child would outside the institution. Older youths who have either completed school or who are no longer required to go to school may be offered the chance to undergo training in some vocational skill that may be useful for finding employment later in life. The manifest reason for behavior modification is to teach the youths about proper behavior through a system that rewards positive behavior and punishes poor behavior. A more cynical view of behavior modification is that it simply serves to control the youths while in the institution, and any long-term behavioral change is an added bonus. Indeed, most institutions have a very formalized point system that they use. This is often referred to as a token economy, where youths earn tokens or points for good behavior and lose tokens for inappropriate actions. The tokens can be redeemed for extra privileges or goods.

Beyond these three interventions, institutions may implement a wide range of additional programming. Individual, group, and family counseling are popular interventions used in institutions, along with drug or alcohol programs, work release, vocational counseling, and job placement. Many training schools use *guided group interaction* as a main form of counseling. This approach relies on the youths to identify problem behaviors, confront one another about their past actions, offer acceptable alternatives to deviant responses, and provide peer pressure to change the behavior of group members (Bartollas, 1985). The counselor or leader tries to remain neutral in the sessions and should guide the discussion with only a minimum of input. Another popular treatment approach is *reality therapy* (which is also used outside the institution by probation programs). Reality therapy emphasizes getting the youths to recognize what they have done and how it affects other people, and to take responsibility for their actions (Glasser, 1965). As with guided group interaction, the hope is that participating youths will find ways to respond to different situations that do not entail harming other people or breaking the law. Psychodrama is a form of treatment that uses role playing as a means of showing youths the effect of their actions from a variety of perspectives. The assumption is that if youths recognize the impact of their actions, they will try to change. The role playing also teaches the appropriate response to different situations. A wide range of other treatment modalities are also used in institutions. It is important to note that, with very few exceptions, the emphasis today is on helping the youth overcome the problems and situations that lead to delinquent activities.

A key issue facing institutional programming is its effectiveness at reducing recidivism and helping the youths become productive members of society. Unfortunately, the evidence on effectiveness, both for youths and adults, is mixed (see Whitehead & Lab, 1999). The reason for this is not entirely clear, although a large part of the problem may entail the degree to which intervention is appropriately implemented and carried out. That is, did the institution deliver the treatment as it was meant to be delivered and at a level sufficient to bring about a positive change? Many studies have failed to find any positive influence of institutional programs on delinquent youth in the aggregate. This means that, when considering changes across a large number of youths, there is little evidence of improvement. At the same time, there may be some individuals who benefit from the programming, but they are not in the majority and do not influence the overall results. One group of advocates for correctional interventions noted that, if the right treatment is applied to the appropriate individuals in the sufficient dosage, treatment is effective (Andrews et al., 1990). The problem is that most interventions, as implemented, do not meet those requirements and, thus, fail to have an impact on many individuals.

Questions over the efficacy of correctional institutions have led to the development of various alternatives in recent years. *Boot camps* have become a popular alternative to traditional training schools. Also known as *shock incarceration,* boot camps are short-term programs that are supposed to handle first-time, nonviolent offenders. The camps are operated on a military model, with strict rules and discipline, physical training and conditioning, counseling, and education (Cronin, 1994). The camps are supposed to show youths that, with hard work and self-discipline, they can succeed in life and do not need to turn to delinquent or criminal behavior. The effect of juvenile boot camps on recidivism, however, is not good, with most evaluations showing little or no change in delinquent behavior (Peters et al., 1997). Despite this fact, boot camps remain a popular alternative, possibly because they take a tough stance and mix physical punishment with the treatment activities. They clearly fit the "get tough on crime" movement in the United States over the past 15 years.

Another approach is *wilderness programming,* in which youths are placed in situations where they must learn survival skills and rely on one another to succeed. These programs can be either short-term or long-term and can take a variety of different forms, including sailing trips, wagon trains, or back-country camps. The underlying idea is to build self-esteem and show the youths that hard work and perseverance pay off. Implicit in the approach is that the skills and self-esteem developed in the program can be transferred back into the daily lives of the youths. Research on these approaches is relatively limited and no clear-cut conclusions can be drawn on their effectiveness. In addition, these programs can be very costly, and there have been problems with serious injuries and even death occurring in the programs.

Another response to concerns over institutional programs is the idea of *deinstitutionalization.* The idea of removing youths from secure institutions, as well as removing them from the purview of the juvenile justice system, received its greatest boost from the 1967 President's Commission on Law Enforcement and the Administration of Justice and the growth of labeling theory in the 1970s. Both the Commission and labeling theory argued that involvement in the juvenile justice system was criminogenic (i.e., it causes crime) and that it was in the best interests of juveniles to keep them out of the system if at all possible. Coupled with the lack of clear reductions in recidivism from system involvement and the escalating costs of dealing with great numbers of juveniles, deinstitutionalization became one attractive alternative. The most noteworthy example of deinstitutionalization in action took place in Massachusetts in the 1970s. Under the leadership of Jerome Miller, Massachusetts closed all of its state-run training schools. What emerged was a system of community-based programs and the placement of serious offenders in private residential settings. Other states followed suit (although to a lesser extent) and moved to less secure methods for handling problem youths (Krisberg and Austin 1993).

Although the deinstitutionalization in Massachusetts and other states was driven by concerns over the effectiveness and costs of residential placement, deinstitutionalization was mandated by the 1974 Juvenile Justice and Delinquency Prevention Act. A major part of this legislation was to remove status offenders from any form of secure confinement. The rationale for this was twofold. First, mixing status offenders and delinquents (those committing criminal acts) has the potential of causing the status offenders more harm than good. Second, status offenders have committed no transgressions against other individuals. Rather, they have exhibited behavior that may lead to problems in the future. Given the possible criminogenic effects of system intervention, it would be in the best interests of the youth to keep them out of any institutional placement. Interestingly, the legislation could not directly force states to deinstitutionalize status offenses, because the states have the legislative authority over this matter. In order to influence the states, however, the legislation mandated withholding federal monies from jurisdictions that failed to deinstitutionalize status offenders. Today, only a small percentage of all youths held in some type of institution are there for status offenses. Instead, most jurisdictions strive to use the *least restrictive placement* that serves both the interests of the youths and the community.

Community Interventions

At the outset of the juvenile justice system in 1899, community interventions were the preferred method for dealing with youths in need of assistance. There were no residential institutions under the control of the court, and the court relied on probation as the primary means of dealing with youths in need of help. Keeping the juvenile at home and in the community was considered the best way of helping children.

Today, community interventions can take a variety of forms, although the most common remains probation. Probation departments are active throughout the juvenile system. Often they fulfill the duties of intake, staff and administer local detention facilities, run informal intervention programs (such as counseling and theft offender programs), and develop *social-history reports* (i.e., the juvenile system equivalent of a presentence investigation). They also make recommendations to the judge on dispositions, as well as work with youths placed on probation. Probation in the juvenile justice system mirrors the process in the adult system. The biggest difference, however, is a greater emphasis on providing treatment and aid to the youths and a reduced interest in simply monitoring and enforcing rules.

Juvenile justice also has a form of parole, commonly referred to as *aftercare*. Aftercare differs from probation mainly by the fact that youths in aftercare have spent some amount of time in a secure facility and are being released back into the community. Many of the rules, regulations, and programming available in aftercare are identical to those found in probation. Consequently, in many communities, aftercare is provided by the probation department. Both probation and aftercare use many of the same treatment ideas, including reality therapy, behavior modification, an emphasis on educational achievement, and vocational training.

Other common community-based interventions are restitution and restorative justice. *Restitution* asks that offenders directly compensate victims for the harm that was caused (Galaway, 1981). The restitution may come in the form of cash or it may involve the juvenile doing some type of work for the victim. If the youth does not have the finances to make monetary restitution or the victim does not want the youth around, some jurisdictions allow the youth to work for the community to make money and pay the victim on behalf of the offender (referred to as *community service restitution*). Proponents of restitution claim that it helps to restore victims to their precrime state, while showing juveniles the harm that they have caused. *Restorative justice* takes a broader approach to helping the victim, by incorporating the needs of the victim, the offender, and the community into the calculation (Bazemore & Maloney, 1994). The term reflects the desire to "restore" all parties to the precrime state. One common approach is to have the juvenile, the victim, the families of the juvenile and victim, and a representative of the community (often from the court) sit down and discuss what took place, the ramifications of the actions, and the best way of resolving the situation for everyone. The restorative justice model has received a great deal of support across the country because it addresses the needs of all parties, and not just the needs of the offender.

Questions of effectiveness for community interventions are similar to those found with institutional interventions. Many programs have exhibited positive results for some youths, especially when the program has been properly implemented and the proper amount of intervention has been applied. What has not been found is any one program that works all the time. In general, programs tend to be time and place specific.

Special Topics

There is a wide range of issues and topics related to youthful misbehavior with which the juvenile justice system must deal on a regular basis. Some of the more prevalent issues are gang behavior, drug use by juveniles, firearms violence, and capital punishment of juveniles. There have also been calls to eliminate the juvenile justice system. Although space does not permit a full discussion of these issues, each is briefly addressed in the following paragraphs.

Gangs

The prevalence and role of gangs have a long history in the juvenile justice system. A major reason for this is the observation that youths tend to commit offenses when in the company of other youths. Some authors have suggested a *group hazard hypothesis* that claims that society responds to group transgressions more than to individual violations (Erickson, 1973).

The study of juvenile gangs dates back to work done in Chicago in the 1930s. Since that time, a wide range of definitions for a gang has emerged, and writers have not settled on a single definition. Typical definitions include reference to a group that identifies itself as a gang, has a name, is recognized by outsiders as a gang, participates in criminal activity, and has some degree of permanence (i.e., it continues over time) (Curry & Decker, 1998). While all gangs do not look alike, there are some common features of most gangs. Most gangs draw youths from the lower classes, are racially homogeneous, offer their members a sense of belonging and status, and are dominated by youths in their late teens. The degree of organization and the behavior of gangs vary considerably, although most gangs are involved in some type of criminal activity. Physical aggression (or the willingness to use physical force) has long been a cornerstone of gang activity, although in recent years this aggression has increasingly featured the use of firearms and has resulted in the death of combatants. Drive-by shootings, or *forays,* have become a recognized part of gang violence in many cities.

Interventions with gangs have taken a variety of forms. At one extreme are strong law enforcement responses, such as the Los Angeles Police Department's Community Resources Against Street Hoodlums (*CRASH*) program, which seeks to disrupt the daily activity of gangs, make arrests, and incarcerate gang members. Legislatures also tend to take a heavy-handed approach and pass laws that make membership in gangs a crime, such as California's Street Terrorism Enforcement and Prevention Act of 1988 (the *STEP Act*). At the other extreme are efforts to interject workers into the daily activity of gangs in hopes of redirecting the gang's activities. A well-known effort of this kind is the *Detached Worker Program.* Unfortunately, there has been little evidence that any of these approaches has had an appreciable impact on gang participation in the United States (Lundman, 1993). One of the most recent attempts to address gangs has been to reach youths before they become gang members and to provide them with the tools to resist the lure of gangs. The *Gang Resistance Education and Training (G.R.E.A.T.)* program involves using police officers to teach antigang, antiviolence lessons in middle schools. Early evaluations of the program show some promising results, although it is not clear if the program has a significant long-term impact on ganging (Esbensen & Osgood, 1997).

Drugs and Delinquency

Drug use by juveniles is considered to be a problem that has grown out of control. The reality is that, except for alcohol and tobacco, very few juveniles use drugs with any frequency, with less than 5 percent reporting the use of drugs within a 30-day period. The evidence suggests that most drug use involves experimentation, rather than consistent use. While this does not mean that drug use is not a problem, it does indicate that the common view of rampant use is not correct. However, drug use is highly related to the commission of other deviant acts and is itself illegal. Data from the *Arrestee Drug Abuse Monitoring (ADAM)* program show that over 50 percent of the arrested youths in most cities test positive for recent drug use.

Responses to youthful drug use and abuse mirror the responses found in adult settings. Typical responses with youths include *detoxification* (weaning a person from addiction), *therapeutic communities* (providing a structured, supportive setting for changing a person's self-esteem and behavior), and various prevention programs. Perhaps the most recognized drug prevention program is the *Drug Abuse Resistance Education (D.A.R.E.)* program. Like G.R.E.A.T., D.A.R.E. is a law enforcement-taught curriculum offered in schools over the course of 17 weeks. The idea is to teach youths about drugs, how to resist peer pressure and how to manage problems like stress, and to build the self-esteem and assertiveness of the youths. Unfortunately, evaluations of D.A.R.E. have found no impact of the program on subsequent drug use (Rosenbaum et al. 1994). Another prevention approach is *skills training,* which involves teaching youths personal and social skills that are useful in making appropriate decisions throughout life and for resisting the lure of deviant activities. Research on skills training has shown positive results, particularly in relation to the use of tobacco, alcohol, and marijuana. The high-profile *"Just Say No"* campaign of the 1980s relied on a very simplistic premise and had virtually no impact on drug use. However, it does illustrate the great interest in antidrug issues among the public.

Capital Punishment and Juveniles

The appropriateness of capital punishment for juveniles has been a matter of debate for several years. This is particularly true since the rise in lethal violence by youths in the late 1980s and early 1990s. Between 1973 and 2000, almost 200 individuals have been sentenced to death for crimes committed when the offender was a juvenile, and 15 offenders were age 15 at the time of the crime (Streib, 2000). A total of 23 states permit the imposition of the death penalty for those who committed their crimes while a juvenile. Although legal challenges to the use of the death penalty for youths persist, the U.S. Supreme Court has ruled that imposing the death penalty for a crime committed when the offender was age 16 or 17 was *not* unconstitutional (*Stanford v. Kentucky,* 1989). The strongest argument against the use of the death penalty for youths revolves around the *parens patriae* philosophy and the belief that youths cannot form the requisite intent in criminal cases. The death penalty ignores the belief that youthful misbehavior is caused by factors beyond the control of the youth.

Calls to Eliminate the Juvenile System

The most extreme suggestion made for the future of the juvenile justice system is to eliminate it (see Feld, 1993). Proponents of this move call for the adult criminal system to assume responsibility for all juvenile transgressions. The underlying reason for this movement is the growth of serious juvenile crime and the inability of the juvenile system to rehabilitate serious offenders. In essence, the call is to return to the same system that was abandoned in 1899.

In some respects, there has been a steady erosion of the *parens patriae* approach in recent years. The use of transfer to the adult system has increased, and states have made transfer a mandatory action for some offenses. There has been a move toward mandatory incarceration for some offenders, and blended sentences are being used with more frequency. The police are now permitted to fingerprint and photograph youthful offenders, and these records are now kept for future reference. Juvenile records are even available to adult courts for consideration in future cases, something that was unheard of 20 years ago.

Despite these changes, there remains a general belief in the need to help youths rather than punish them. Consequently, eliminating the juvenile justice system makes little sense. Feld (1993) argues that the adult system would have to make drastic changes if it were to assume responsibility for juvenile offenders. Many of the changes would probably mirror the current activities of the juvenile system. What is needed is a system that has the flexibility to provide the due process rights needed to protect the accused and the power to use whatever intervention is in the best interests of both the offender and society. Clearly, the juvenile justice system will continue to undergo change and that change may include moving closer to the adult system.

References

Andrews, D. A., Zinger, I., Hoge, R. D., Bonta, J., Gendreau, P., & Cullen, F. T. (1990). Does correctional treatment work? A clinically relevant and psychologically informed meta-analysis. *Criminology, 28*(4), 369–404.

Bartollas, C. (1985). *Correctional treatment: Theory and practice.* Englewood Cliffs, NJ: Prentice Hall.

Bazemore, G., & Maloney, D. (1994). Rehabilitating community service: Toward restorative service sanctions in a balanced justice system. *Federal Probation, 58*(1), 24–35.

Butts, J. A., Snyder, H. N., Finnegan, T. A., Aughenbaugh, A. L., Tierney, N. J., Sullivan, D. P., Poole, R. S., Sickmund, M. S., & Poe, E. C. (1994). *Juvenile court statistics, 1991.* Washington, DC: U.S. Department of Justice.

Commonwealth v. Fisher, 213 Pa. 48 (1905).

Cronin, R. C. (1994). *Boot camps for adult and juvenile offenders: Overview and update.* Washington, DC: National Institute of Justice.

Curry, G. D., & Decker, S. H. (1998). *Confronting gangs: Crime and community.* Los Angeles: Roxbury Publishing.

Erickson, M. L. (1973). Group violations and official delinquency: The group hazard hypothesis. *Criminology, 11*(1), 127–160.

Esbensen, F., & Osgood, D. W. (1997). *National evaluation of G.R.E.A.T.: NIJ research in brief.* Washington, DC: National Institute of Justice.

Ex parte Crouse, 4 Wheaton (Pa.) 9 (1838).

Feld, B. C. (1993). *Justice for children: The right to counsel and the juvenile courts.* Boston: Northeastern University Press.

Galaway, B. (1981). The use of restitution. In B. Galaway and J. Hudson (Eds.), *Perspectives on crime victims.* St. Louis, MO: Mosby.

Glasser, W. (1965). *Reality therapy.* New York: Harper and Row.

In re Gault, 387 U.S. 187 S. Ct. 1428, 18 L.Ed.2d 527 (1967).

In re Winship, 397 U.S. 358, 90 S. Ct. 1068, 25 L. Ed. 2d 368 (1970).

Kent v. United States, 383 U.S. 541, 86 S. Ct. 1045, 16 L.Ed.2d 84 (1966).

Krisberg, B., & Austin, J. F. (1993). *Reinventing juvenile justice.* Newbury Park, CA: Sage.

Lundman, R. J. (1993). *Prevention and control of juvenile delinquency* (2nd ed.). New York: Oxford.

McKeiver v. Pennsylvania, 403 U.S. 528, 91 S.Ct. 1976, 29 L.Ed.2d 647 (1971).

Peters, M., Thomas, D., & Zamberlan, C. (1997). *Boot camps for juvenile offenders: Program summary.* Washington, DC: U.S. Department of Justice.

Pisciotta, A. W. (1983). Race, sex, and rehabilitation: A study of differential treatment in the juvenile reformatory, 1825–1900. *Crime and Delinquency, 29,* 254–269.

President's Commission on Law Enforcement and the Administration of Justice. (1967). *Task force report: Juvenile delinquency and youth crime.* Washington, DC: Government Printing Office.

Rosenbaum, D. P., Flewelling, R. L., Bailey, S. L., Ringwalt, C. L., & Wilkinson, D. L. (1994). Cops in the classroom: A longitudinal evaluation of Drug Abuse Resistance Education (DARE). *Journal of Research in Crime and Delinquency, 31*(1), 3–31.

Rossum, R. A., Koller, B. J., & Manfredi, C. P. (1987). *Juvenile justice reform: A model for the states.* Claremont, CA: Rose Institute of State and Local Government.

Schall v. Martin, 467 U.S. 253, 104 S.Ct. 2403, 81 L.Ed.2d (1984).

Sickmund, M. (1994). How juveniles get to criminal court. *Juvenile Justice Bulletin.* Washington, DC: U.S. Department of Justice.

Sickmund, M. (1997). *Offenders in juvenile court, 1995.* Washington, DC: U.S. Department of Justice.

Silberman, C. E. (1978). *Criminal violence, crime justice.* New York: Random House.

Snyder, H. N., & Sickmund, M. H. (1999). *Juvenile offenders and victims: 1999 national report.* Washington, DC: Office of Juvenile Justice and Delinquency Prevention.

Stanford v. Kentucky, 492 U.S. 361 (1989).

Streib, V. L. (2000). *The juvenile death penalty today: Death sentences and executions for juvenile crimes, January 1, 1973–June 30, 2000.* Ada: Ohio Northern University, Claude W. Pettit College of Law.

Torbet, P., Gable, R., Hurst, H., Montgomery, I., Szymanski, L., & Thomas, D. (1996). *State responses to serious and violent juvenile crime.* Washington, DC: Office of Juvenile Justice and Delinquency Prevention.

Whitehead, J. T., & Lab, S. P. (1999). *Juvenile justice: An introduction* (3rd ed.). Cincinnati, OH: Anderson.

Suggested Readings

General Juvenile Justice

Whitehead, J. T., & Lab, S. P. (1999). *Juvenile justice: An introduction* (3rd ed.). Cincinnati, OH: Anderson.

History

Empy, L. T. (1982). *American delinquency: Its meaning and construction.* Homewood, IL: Dorsey Press. Chapters 2–4.

Transfer or Waiver

Sickmund, M. (1994). How juveniles get to criminal court. *Juvenile Justice Bulletin.* Washington, DC: U.S. Department of Justice.

Changing Philosophy

Feld, B. C. (1993). *Justice for children: The right to counsel and the juvenile courts.* Boston: Northeastern University Press.

Krisberg, B., & Austin, J. F. (1993). *Reinventing juvenile justice.* Newbury Park, CA: Sage.

Torbet, P., Gable, R., Hurst, H., Montgomery, I., Szymanski, L., & Thomas, D. (1996). *State responses to serious and violent juvenile crime.* Washington, DC: Office of Juvenile Justice and Delinquency Prevention.

Discussion Questions

1. What are some of the major concerns that decision makers should consider when deciding how to proceed with juvenile offenders? What considerations should be paramount and why?

2. What are the consequences of increasingly treating juveniles as adults in the criminal justice system? Do you think this is a positive development? Why or why not? ✦

Readings for Further Topics

Crime Prevention

Clarke, R. V. (1997). *Situational crime prevention: Successful case studies* (2nd ed.). Guilderland, NY: Harrow and Heston.

Hughes, G., McLaughlin, E., & Muncie, J. (2002). *Crime prevention and community safety: New directions.* Thousand Oaks, CA: Sage.

Lab, S. P. (2000). *Crime prevention: Approaches, practices, and evaluation.* Cincinnati, OH: Anderson.

Rosenbaum, D. P., & Lurigio, A. J. (1998). *The prevention of crime: Social and situational strategies.* Belmont, CA: Wadsworth.

Victimology

Doerner, W. G., & Lab, S. P. (2002). *Victimology* (3rd ed.). Cincinnati, OH: Anderson.

Kennedy, L. W., & Sacco, V. F. (1998). *Crime victims in context.* Los Angeles: Roxbury Publishing.

Restorative Justice

Bazemore, G., & Schiff, M. (Eds.). (2001). *Restorative community justice: Repairing harm and transforming communities.* Cincinnati, OH: Anderson.

Braithwaithe, J. (2002). *Restorative justice and responsive regulation.* New York: Oxford University Press.

Johnstone, G. (2001). *Restorative justice: Ideas, values, debates.* Portland, OR: Willan Publishing

Terrorism

Griset, P., & Mahan, S. (Eds.). (2002). *Terrorism in perspective.* Thousand Oaks, CA: Sage.

Hudson, R. (1999). *The sociology and psychology of terrorism: Who becomes a terrorist and why.* Washington, DC: Federal Research Division, Library of Congress.

Race, Class, and Gender

Belknap, J. (2001). *The invisible woman: Gender, crime, and justice* (2nd ed.). Belmont, CA: Wadsworth.

Reiman, J. H. (2001). *The rich get richer and the poor get prison: Ideology, class, and criminal justice* (6th ed.). Boston: Allyn and Bacon.

Walker, S., Spohn, C., & DeLone, M. (2000). *The color of justice: Race, ethnicity, and crime in America.* Belmont, CA: Wadsworth.

International Criminal Justice

Reichel, P. L. (2002). *Comparative criminal justice systems: A topical approach.* Upper Saddle River, NJ: Prentice Hall.

Terrill, R. J. (2003). *World criminal justice systems: A survey.* Cincinnati, OH: Anderson.

Tonry, M., & Frase, R. S. (Eds.). (2001). *Sentencing and sanctions in Western countries.* New York: Oxford. ✦

Author Index

A

Abadinsky, H., 134
Adams, K., 124, 126
Ageton, S.S., 44
Agnew, R., 39, 46
Andrews, D.A., 157
Aughenbaugh, A.L., 164
Austin, J., 106, 107
Austin, J.F., 158, 166

B

Bailey, S.L., 165
Bandura, A., 27
Bartollas, C., 156
Bazemore, G., 160, 167
Beck, A., 13, 107, 108
Belknap, J., 168
Bernard, T.J., 46
Bittner, E., 50
Blumstein, A., 13, 107, 108
Bohm, R.M., 46
Bohn, M.J., 29
Bonta, J., 164
Booth, A., 23
Bottoms, A., 124, 126
Braithwaithe, J., 167
Braswell, M., 46
Bryne, J.M., 134
Bucqueroux, B., 80
Bursik, R.J., 30
Butts, J.A., 145

C

Caldero, M.A., 79
Carp, R., 100
Clarke, R.V., 35, 167
Clear, T.R., 120, 129
Cohen, A.K., 33, 34
Cohen, L.E., 35
Cohen, S., 117
Cole, G., 120
Cornish, D.B., 35
Crank, J.P., 72, 79
Cronin, R.C., 157
Cullen, F.T., 6, 13, 46, 164
Curry, G.D., 161

D

Dalton, K., 23
Dammer, H.R., 129
Decker, S.H., 161
DeLone, M., 168
Dinovitzer, R., 129
Ditton, P.M., 111
Doerner, W.G., 167
Donzinger, S.R., 106
Durkheim, E., 39

E

Elliot, D.S., 43
Empy, L.T., 166
Erickson, M.L., 160
Esbensen, F., 161

Subject Index

A

ADAM (Arrestee Drug Abuse Monitoring), 162
Adjudication stage, 149–150
Adolescents. See juveniles
Adoption studies, 22–23
Adult court, transferring juveniles to, 139, 148,–149, 163
Adversarial justice systems, 85
African Americans
    employment in criminal justice system, 12
    police protection of, 67
    racial profiling, 73–74
    strain theory, 40
Aftercare, 159
Age
    death penalty, 162–163
    elderly, 77, 111, 130
    juveniles, defined, 139
    mitigating circumstances, 111
    policing juveniles, 143–144
    sentencing, 150–151
Agencies, police, 52–56, 58
Aggravating circumstances, 110–111
Alcohol use
    genetic factors, 23
    juveniles, 138, 161
    regulations, 55
Alternative dispute resolution, 12, 99
Animal and Plant Health Inspection Service, 56
Anomie, 39

Anonymity, 4
Antiwar movement, 67
Appeals
    federal courts, 90–91
    state courts, 92
    trial process, 99
Appellate jurisdiction, 90–91, 92
Appointed attorneys, 95
Arabs, racial profiling, 78
Arraignments, 98
Arrest, house, 113
Arrestee Drug Abuse Monitoring (ADAM), 162
Arrests
    force, use of, 74–75
    Miranda rights, 12, 66–67
    order maintenance, 51–52
    police discretion, 9, 50, 73, 144
    warrants, 96–97
    zero tolerance policy, 70–71
Assembly–line justice, 88
Assigned counsel, 95
Atavistic qualities, 21
ATF (Bureau of Alcohol, Tobacco, and Firearms), 55
Attorney general, 93
Attorneys
    assembly–line justice, 88
    defense, 94–95, 98–99
    district, 93
    judge supervision, 96
    juvenile court, 149, 150, 151–152
    prosecutors, 93, 97–99

Chief prosecutors, 93
Children. *See also* juveniles
   age of, 139
   bond to society, 36–37
   developmental theory, 26
   differential association theory, 31
   history of legal treatment, 140–143
   learning theory, 27–28
   media, influence on, 32
   self–control theory, 38
CHINS (child in need of service), 139
CIA (Central Intelligence Agency), 56
Circuit courts, 90, 92
Circumstances, affect on sentencing, 110–111
Citizens
   community policing, 68, 69–70
   Neighborhood Watch, 51
   role in criminal justice system, 8, 9
City courts, 92
City police agencies, 53
Civil law
   courts, 91
   defined, 83–84
   state courts, 92
Civil liberties, 78
Civil rights movement, 67
Civil War, impact on court systems, 90, 91
Civilian police staff, 57
Civilian review, police, 76
Civility, 7
Classicism, 19
Classification review, 121
Classifications, crime, 2
Close security prisons, 121–122
Coast Guard, 56
Committees of Vigilance, 64
Common law, 64, 82
Common pleas courts, 92
Commonwealth v. Fisher, 142

Communities
   high–crime neighborhoods, 30
   policing, 31, 52, 66–71
   reintegration of prisoners, 128–129
   role in criminal justice system, 8, 12
   special needs groups, 77
Community interventions, 158–160
Community Resources Against Street Hoodlums (CRASH), 161
Community service restitution, 159–160
Community service work (CSW), 112
Community supervision, 114
Community–oriented policing (COP), 69–71
CompStat, 71
Concurrent sentences, 110
Conditions, probation, 114–115
Confidentiality, 3
Conflict theories, 41–43
Conformity, defined, 39
Consecutive sentences, 110
Consent decrees, 76
Constables, 63
Constitution, U.S.
   Eighth Amendment rights, 86
   Fifth Amendment rights, 66–67, 85–86
   Fourteenth Amendment rights, 85–86, 94
   Fourth Amendment rights, 66
   juvenile justice, 151–152
   laws, interpreting, 83
   Sixth Amendment rights, 94, 151–152
   U.S. Supreme Court, creation of, 89, 91
Constitutions, state, 83
Containment theory, 37
Contraband, 120, 124
Contract cities, 58

I

I–levels, 26
Id, 25–26
Identity theft, 78
Illegal behavior
 defined, 2
 juveniles, 138
Immigrants, language barriers, 75, 77
Immigration and Naturalization Service (INS), 56, 77
Importation model, 126
Imprisonment. See incarceration
In re Gault, 152
In re Winship, 152
Incarceration
 coping with, 125–127
 frequency of, 111
 history of, 104–105
 jails, 119–120
 prisons, 120–123
 rate, 13, 107–108, 129
 reintegration, 128–129
 safety, 123–124
 sentence length, 108
 shock, 113, 157
 types of, 113
Incorrigible, defined, 139
Independent variables, 17
Indeterminate sentencing, 109–111
Indian Affairs, Bureau of, 56
Indictments, 98
Individual liberty, 7
Individualism, 25
Inmates
 drug use, 130
 medical care, 130
 releasing, 127–128
 violence, 124–125
Innocence
 pleas, 97, 98
 presumption of, 98–99
Innovation, defined, 39
INS (Immigration and Naturalization Service), 56, 77
Intake decision, 147

Integration, theory, 43
Intelligence
 Department of Homeland Security, 56
 Metropolitan London Police, 63–64
Intensive Supervision Probation (ISP), 113, 118
Intent, criminal, 141
Intermediate sanctions, 113–119
Interpersonal Maturity Levels, 26
Investigators
 crime, 68
 police, 61, 62
ISP (Intensive Supervision Probation), 113, 118

J

Jails. *See also* prisons
 defined, 119
 functions of, 119–120
 incarceration rate, 107–108
 sentence lengths, 113
John detail, 62
Judges
 adversarial justice systems, 85
 assembly–line justice, 88
 bench trials, 98
 checks and balances, 8
 discretion, 13, 107, 110, 111
 juvenile court, 149
 law interpretation, 81–83
 probation violations, 116
 roles, 95–96
 sentencing, role in, 99
Judicial waiver, 148
Judiciary Act of 1789, 90, 91
Juries
 adversarial justice systems, 85
 death penalty cases, 99
 grand, 97
 judge supervision, 96
 juvenile courts, 153
 trials, 98
Jurisdiction
 age limits, 139
 appellate, 90–91, 92

juvenile justice, 151–152
laws, interpreting, 83
Sixth Amendment rights, 86,
94, 151–152
U.S. Supreme Court, creation of,
89, 91
U.S. Courts of Appeal, 90–91
U.S. Marshals Service, 56, 67
U.S. Mint Police, 55
U.S. Supreme Court
creation of, 89–90
defense attorneys, 94
jurisdiction, 91
juvenile justice, rulings on,
143, 151–153, 163
UCR (Uniform Crime Reports), 3,
18, 66
Unanimous juries, 98
Unconscious drives, 25
Undercover police, 62
Uniform Crime Reports (UCR), 3,
18, 66
Uniformed police officers, 57
Unions, 64–65, 76
Unruly, defined, 139
Utopian societies, 6

V

Validity, 18
Values, subcultures, 33–34
Variables, 17–18
Verdicts, 98–99
Victimization statistics, 2, 4, 140
Victims
reporting crimes, 3, 9
restorative justice, 159–160
Vietnam War, 67
Vigilantes, 64
Violations, probation, 115–116,
117, 118, 119
Violence, inmate, 124–125
Viscerotonic temperament, 22
Vocational counseling, 155, 156

Vollmer, August, 65
Volunteers
community service work
(CSW), 112
police, 54

W

Waivers, of juveniles to adult
courts, 139, 148–149, 163
War on drugs, 107
Warrants, 96–97
Watch, the, 63
Weapons, police use of, 74–75
Wickersham Commission, 65
Wilderness programing, 157
Wilson, O.W., 65
Winship, In re, 152
Witness Protection Program, 56
Witnesses, defendant rights, 85, 86
Women
employment in criminal
justice system, 12, 57, 72
feminist theory, 42
prisoners, 105, 122, 125
Work release, 113, 119
Workgroup, courtroom, 88
World Trade Center attacks
Department of Homeland
Security, 56
policing, affects on, 77–78
special police, 54
Wrongful use of force, 74

Y

Youthful offender statutes, 139,
151
Youths. *See* juveniles

Z

Zero tolerance policy, 68, 70-71✦